THE MAGICAL GIRL'S GUIDE TO LIFE

FIND YOUR INNER POWER, FIGHT EVERYDAY
EVIL & SAVE THE DAY WITH SELF-CARE

BY JACQUE AYE

ULYSSES PRESS

Published in the US by:
ULYSSES PRESS
PO Box 3440
Berkeley, CA 94703
www.ulyssespress.com

ISBN: 978-1-64604-248-7
Library of Congress Control Number: 2021937733

Printed in the United States by Versa Press
10 9 8 7 6 5 4 3 2 1

Acquisitions editor: Casie Vogel
Managing editor: Claire Chun
Project editor: Tyanni Niles
Editor: Renee Rutledge
Proofreader: Barbara Schultz
Front cover design: Kristine Byun
Interior design: what!design @ whatweb.com
Layout: Jake Flaherty
Interior artwork: Venus Bambisa
Author photograph: Jacque Aye

NOTE TO READERS: This book is independently authored and published and no sponsorship or endorsement of this book by, and no affiliation with, any celebrities, television shows, movies, characters, or trademarked products mentioned or pictured within is claimed or suggested. All celebrities, television shows, movies, characters, or trademarked products that appear in this book belong to their respective owners and are used here for informational purposes only. The author and publisher encourage readers to patronize the quality shows, movies, and other products mentioned and pictured in this book.

CONTENTS

INTRODUCTION

> **❝Have you ever wished you were a magical girl?❞**

I was born and raised in the grayest, flattest place you could imagine, smack-dab in the middle of the country—Kansas. I actually don't know why my parents chose Kansas as their new locale after leaving their homes in Nigeria, but that's where they ended up, and that's where I lived for most of my life. No offense to my fellow Kansans, of course; they're some of the absolute best people, who just happen to live in a very flat place.

Now, before you ask, yes, I've seen *The Wizard of Oz*, and yes, I've tried clicking my heels together on numerous occasions, not to go back home, but hoping to escape the drudgery of life. Even as a kid I wished I had the power to click my heels or snap my fingers and inject my mundane life with a bit of magic. I'd simply *snap and click* and there'd be an insanely cute, ambiguous-looking creature before me, saying, "Ah, I've been searching for you for so long!" before whisking me away on some otherworldly adventure. Maybe I'd find I was actually a princess of a lost kingdom, or maybe my house would end up flattening a witch. Either way, it would've been much more interesting than waking up, filling my day with seemingly meaningless tasks, and then laying my head on my pillow at night, fighting my insomnia monsters. But no matter how hard I snapped or how feverishly I clicked my heels, nothing changed. Instead, I trudged through life, head down and nose firmly planted between the pages of whatever fantasy book I chose to escape into, hoping for more.

The older I grew, the slower I trudged and the more the prospect of everyday magic seemed to fade from my consciousness until it was almost completely gone. But one day I had a realization that changed everything. No, there wasn't a magical snap that whisked me away to a faraway land, but something did *click*. One day I declared to myself, and to everyone I knew, that *I was a magical girl*.

I have a sneaking suspicion that since you've picked up this book you're at least familiar with the world of magical girls. But in case you aren't, here's a rundown. The magical girl genre, also known as *mahou shoujo*, originated in Japan as far back as the 1960s with the beloved anime *Sally the Witch*. The genre gained massive popularity in the 1990s and early 2000s through series like *Sailor Moon* and *Cardcaptor Sakura*. Magical girl influences eventually reached around the globe and inspired Western shows like *Winx Club*, *Miraculous: Tales of Ladybug & Cat Noir*, *Steven Universe*, and *Star vs. the Forces of Evil*.

But what *is* a magical girl, you ask? To put it simply, magical girls are weapon-wielding, adorable costume-wearing, crime-fighting cuties! They're often accompanied by an anthropomorphic furry familiar, and together, they fight bad guys, using magic, in the name of friendship and love. In the world of magical girls, unlike the real world, femininity, emotional openness, and softness are associated with power, intelligence, and strength. You don't have to take on "masculine" traits to be taken seriously, and there's no dramatic "makeunder" to dull down your sparkle in order to gain the respect of your foes and peers. As you become more powerful, you become even more glamorous. That's what I love most about the genre. Magical girls aren't always "girls" either. *Any* magical being can don a stylish costume and fight for a better, more caring world.

My first brush with the genre was back in the '90s, when my brother would turn on *Sailor Moon* and I'd silently poke my head out from my blanket and watch along in awe. The five Sailor Senshi, or guardians of the solar system, were like Power Rangers. They'd kick monster butt on a weekly basis while attending school and crushing over classmates. But unlike Power Rangers, the girls dressed and acted just like me. The pleated skirts, bows, and ruffles resembled the outfits my mom would pick for me before sending me off into the world. Usagi, the main character, would cry and question her every move—not unlike myself. Her friend Ami was intelligent and capable, but also shy and reserved, which resonated with me. It was like looking into a mirror and seeing myself on-screen in ways I hadn't seen before. Mind you, I was extremely young, but the show made a lasting impact on me. I was fixated on their elaborate magical transformations and wanted nothing more than to wear heels and nail polish just like them.

At the time, magical girls were just fashionable cartoon characters that I enjoyed watching every week, but it took me many years of personal struggles before I realized there was much more beneath their glamorous exterior. Once I consciously took on those magical girl traits and applied them to myself in real, tangible ways, everything changed! I found myself, I found my community, and my existence became more than just a constant trudging. While life can still be dull, as life tends to be, I've finally found how to inject a bit of magic into it through mindfulness, friendship, purpose, and love. And while I do have a furry sidekick, my adorable, adopted pup Nala, I didn't even need her to tell me I was the lost princess of another dimension. I simply found my power within.

With that inner power, I went on to create a six-figure e-commerce business. I created a universe full of magical characters, wrote my first manga-inspired comic book, and invited everyone to enter my world. To my delight, tens of thousands of people did. I went from a lonely, awkward girl to, well, a still-awkward woman but with a community of over one hundred thousand magical beings across social media. And I still manage to find time for self-care because nothing is more important than peace of mind. While my business has been an amazing accomplishment, the true heart of my journey was strengthening my friendships and finding ways to defeat my formidable weekly adversary—social anxiety.

If you're wondering if you'd be able to wield the same life-changing power to add a bit of magic to your mundane life, the answer is *absolutely*. This book will serve as your official guide to becoming the most magical version of yourself here in the real world. You'll learn a lot about me, even the ugly, ordinary parts. I'll be sharing my highest highs and lowest lows because they seem to go hand in hand, and because I want you to see what goes on behind the veil. In the process you'll learn much more about yourself, your monsters, and how to defeat them with your newfound magical powers! Of course there will be personality quizzes and lessons from your favorite magical girls woven in for good measure as well. Throughout the book, I may mention a few potentially new terms, so if you find yourself wondering what exactly a Magical Girl Identifier Index is, for example, just flip to our Official Magical Girl Glossary on page 187.

MAGICAL GIRL REQUIREMENTS
(in no particular order)

Anyone can be a magical girl! But there is a distinct set of requirements.

1. A big heart and a desire to help others.

2. A sense of optimism, even in the face of mounting challenges.

3. Self-awareness and a spirit of discernment.

4. A magical moniker.

5. A faithful furry sidekick.

6. An arsenal of personalized weapons to cut down your adversaries.

7. A desire to build meaningful, long-lasting friendships.

8. A transformation sequence.*

9. A love of love.

10. And, of course, a magical power!

* As with everything in life, this rule has some exceptions. Not every magical girl has an elaborate, outfit-changing transformation sequence, but every magical girl fights in a fabulous and powerful outfit!

DO YOU HAVE WHAT IT TAKES?

Even if you have a strong desire to become a magical girl, you may not be entirely sure how to go about embodying the spirit of fictional characters in the real world. Well, no worries! I'm happy to act as your stand-in familiar, guiding you through life, sharing lessons to help you embrace the more magical side of yourself. But before we get started, ask yourself these questions to see if you qualify for magical endowment:

- Are you a bit clumsy?

- Do people think you can be emotional?

- Are you shy or nervous to be yourself around others?

- Have you often felt out of place?

If the answer to any of these questions is "yes," then you have what it takes to become a magical being. I know what you're thinking. None of those traits sound very remarkable. In fact, they seem like hindrances, and magical girls are extraordinary, powerful beings. But what if I told you that underneath the surface, you're secretly bursting at the seams with untapped magic? Or that monsters flock to you because you're buzzing with an excess of powerful energy?

Understanding how to apply magical girl logic to real-world scenarios takes a bit of reframing of what you know magic to be. Spells, sparkles, and incantations are accurate portrayals of magic on glowing screens and in the black-and-white pages of manga. But in the real-world, magic doesn't just appear in a bright flash of light. It's quiet. It's subtle. And if you don't slow down to pay attention, you'll miss it. Close your eyes for a second and think about the last happy moment you shared with a friend. Now, imagine a time you overcame a challenging experience and reveled in your triumph. Did you catch that fleeting feeling of warmth and joy as you called upon those memories? *That's* magic.

Monsters also take on a different form in the real world than they do in the fantastical world of magical girls. Your personal adversary is not a stunning but terrifying redhead with an amazing sense of style. No, monsters in the real world are invisible. They take the form of feelings like anxiety, impostor syndrome, and self-sabotage to attack you from within. These monsters prey on your fears and can possess you if left to grow more powerful.

These may be hard concepts to grasp without proper training, I know. But that's what I'm here for. By the end of this guide, you'll be an expert on the matters of real-world magic and monsters. You'll be so full of wisdom and knowledge that you won't even need me, and you'd be able to write this book yourself. Blindfolded. Now that you know you've got what it takes to don your elaborate costume and wield your weapon of love and justice, let's dive into discovering your unique inner power.

ONE

WHAT'S YOUR MAGICAL GIRL POWER?

The first step on your journey to becoming a bona fide magical being is finding and defining your power. Every fictional magical being seems to stumble upon their power in similar ways. In the powerhouse magical girl anime *Sailor Moon*, Usagi Tsukino is your average fourteen-year-old girl. She's a bit of a crybaby who loves her friends, loves food, and struggles to complete her homework assignments. But after saving Luna, a curious black cat, from a group of mischievous children, Usagi learns that she's destined to become Sailor Moon—the Pretty Guardian of Love and Justice. She's then tasked with finding the rest of the Sailor Senshi, locating the missing Moon Princess Serenity, and saving the world. Usagi thinks she's dreaming at first, as anyone would when talking to a cat that talks back, but it doesn't take much convincing once Luna gives her a shiny transformation broach and she hears her friend Naru in distress. Her quick acceptance of her power doesn't mean she's without struggle. Throughout the series, she battles self-doubt, fear, and defeat. But she fights through her feelings with the help of Luna and her best friends.

In the French series *Miraculous: Tales of Ladybug & Cat Noir*, a somewhat clumsy young girl named Marinette Dupain-Cheng and a wealthy, isolated boy (Adrien Agreste) with an overbearing father gain the power of creation and destruction after "finding" a pair of ladybug earrings and a cat-shaped ring. In reality, the magical jewelry, referred to as "Miraculous," was planted by Master Wang Fu, the guardian of the Miraculouses. He knows the teens are strong enough, and compassionate enough, to wield the power of the Miraculouses and save the world. Marinette and Adrien transform under the guidance of their kwamis, or magical familiars, and they become Ladybug and Cat Noir. Adrien jumps into action and assumes his new title enthusiastically but, after their first battle goes terribly wrong, Marinette takes a little time and an extra push to truly step into her power. Once she does embrace her magic, she's unstoppable! At least, when she's costumed up. As Marinette, she still struggles with the confidence to live up to her powerful secret identity.

You can see the overlap in each magical girl's journey. Both Usagi and Marinette are regular, albeit clumsy, girls who are chosen to save the world from the forces of evil with guidance from their familiars. As magical girls, they still struggle with the self-doubt and fear that come with the responsibility of bearing such an incredible power. They deal with the same impostor syndrome that we all face when being thrust into a new role with much more on our plate. As you read through this guide and embrace your magic, it will be uncomfortable at times. You'll doubt yourself and worry if you're really meant to wield your power. *But you are.* Like Usagi and Marinette, you've been chosen to embark on this path!

Every magical being on this planet has a special power that's unique to them, and while it may not be as fantastical as a super-powered yo-yo, *trust me*, it's just as mighty. While I've never stumbled upon any ancient power granting objects myself, my magical girl power appeared pretty early on, but it took me many years of trial and error to truly embrace and understand it. Similar to Marinette, I was a bit reluctant to take on my magical girl mantle, and just like Usagi, I cried my way through most of it.

Before we get into the origins of my power, let's uncover yours using a method of magic discovery I've perfected over the years—the Magical Girl Identifier Index, or MGII, as I like to call it. After years of research, I've found that each magical being falls under one of five major categories: Heart, Intelligence, Passion, Strength, and Creativity. The following questions will determine which category suits you best. Answer each question honestly and from the heart. Let your inner magic guide you!

MAGICAL GIRL IDENTIFIER INDEX QUESTIONS

A small, cuddly creature approaches you as you're walking down a crowded street. They're saying that you've been chosen for a very important matter, that you're magical and the world needs you. It's time to don your battle-ready outfit, tap into your inner magic, and save us all! So you:

A. Act on faith, put others before yourself, and wholeheartedly accept the creature's proposal. People need your help, after all, and you can always ask questions later.

B. Discreetly step into an alleyway with the creature and ask as many questions as you can think of to get a clearer understanding of what's going on.

C. Confidently accept the creature's proposal. This is your chance! You've always dreamed of changing the world.

D. Ask the creature to prove it and teach you how to fight. If you really have inner magic, you want to see it in action right away.

E. Freak out and run away. You leave that little critter in the dust but, after some time, you feel unsure and guilty. You go sauntering back to hear them out.

Now that you've accepted your fate, which of these abilities would you choose if you could?

A. An empath with telepathic abilities.

B. A tech wizard who can control energy and electricity.

C. A musical maestro with the ability to bring enemies to their knees with your voice.

D. A hand-to-hand combat expert with fiery sun-powered magic.

E. A magician with the ability to create mind-boggling illusions with the flick of your staff.

It's time for battle! But before you run in swinging, you need to choose an outfit. Which of these outfits is most up your style alley?

A. Full on glitter and glam, nails painted, heels high, and lipstick poppin'!

B. A cute and practical outfit that you can maneuver around in—with pockets. You've got to store those gadgets somewhere!

C. A dramatic ensemble that speaks to who you are—and amplifies it.

D. A sleek outfit that's more function than fashion, but you make it look amazing, as you always do.

E. Why choose just one outfit when you could have a different one for each occasion? Yes, it's a bit laborious but you think it's worth it!

As a magical girl, you know that your team is everything! Who's fighting by your side?

A. Your four best friends, each with their own unique powers.

B. You fight alone until you stumble across a mysterious magical girl you've never seen before. You're intrigued and join forces.

C. Besides the encouraging presence of your familiar, you fight solo dolo. You've got to keep your work and home life separate, you know?

D. You fight beside your more seasoned, more experienced mentor. You watch them in awe as you learn and grow with them.

E. You travel around and team up with new, exciting people everywhere you go.

Your best friend comes to you, head hanging and near tears, explaining how they're being bullied at work. So you:

A. Empathize with your friend then offer them emotional support in the form of a warm hug.

B. Ask follow-up questions then come up with tangible solutions to solve their problem.

C. Tell your friend you're willing to speak to their boss on their behalf.

D. Encourage your friend to stand their ground and stand up to their bully.

E. Help your friend redesign their résumé.

You trip over your own feet and go toppling to the ground. It's embarrassing enough that a handful of strangers see this happening, but you look up and notice your crush staring right at you. They ask, "Are you okay?" with a look of concern in their eyes. So you:

A. Cry from the embarrassment.

B. Assure them that you're fine, and there's no need to worry.

C. Use this as an opportunity to flirt and say, "I'm okay now that you're here."

D. Hop back up and dust yourself off like nothing happened.

E. Answer, "I've been better!" and laugh it off.

Magical beings have a lot on their mind. What keeps you up at night?

A. Thinking of all the people in the world who need your help.

B. Thinking of a problem that arose during the day. You can't sleep until you solve it!

C. Planning out a protest or charity drive.

D. Thinking of how you will optimize your time the next day.

E. Thinking of all the creative ideas swimming around in your head.

Adult magical beings have a lot on their plates. How do you approach your goals?

A. You have a dream and let your heart guide your steps. No need to plan beyond that!

B. Map out your goals and create an extensive plan. You don't like surprises so you eliminate them the best you can.

C. Your goals revolve around helping others, so you just go where you're needed.

D. Approach? You pounce on your goals and grab them by the horns!

E. Instead of goals, your mind is full of amazing ideas and you find it hard to choose just one.

Magical girls fight monsters! Which of these beasts would be your monster of the week?

A. The Anxiety Monster, a hulking beast that preys on the fears of magical beings across the globe.

B. The Sultan of Self-Doubt, a cunning monster that burrows its way into the minds of magical beings, casting illusions of mediocrity and making them doubt their own power.

C. The Master Manipulator, an unhinged genius who uses the power of its mind to mix things up in yours.

D. The Duke of Despair, a harrowing monster that feeds on the misery, sadness, and defeat of its host.

E. The Baron of Boringness, a monster that zaps color and vibrancy from everything it touches. It also creates blocks in the minds of magical beings, stopping them from expressing themselves.

How would you defeat your monsters?

A. Make an emotional plea and try to change their heart through love and compassion.

B. Use logic to reason with them. Instead of spending all their energy fighting you, they could be making lucrative investments or pursuing their own fulfilling passions.

C. Zap them into another dimension where they can't hurt anyone anymore.

D. Tire them out. You could do this all day!

E. Scare them. Act so strange and out of character that they get confused and give up.

Adulting is hard. And so is fighting monsters. What do you do to unwind after a long day of battling bad guys?

A. Do a face mask, light a candle, then cry. But just a little. Except on those days when you cry a lot.

B. Play video games. Something about strategizing and leveling up in a virtual world just calms your nerves.

C. Snuggle up under a blanket with your phone, grab a snack, check social media, and connect with others across the world.

D. Hit the gym and release your stress through physical activity.

E. Pull out a notebook or sketchbook, and create.

ANSWER KEY

Time to tally up! Let's see where your power lies...

MOSTLY A'S: If you answered mostly A's, your magical girl power falls under the **Heart** category. Magical beings with heart put others before themselves. They make it a mission in life to help other people feel safe and warm, and they're willing to sacrifice their own personal comfort in order to make the world a better place. Magical beings with heart may stumble through friendships and relationships, but only because they care too much and end up in more trouble than they bargained for when trying to please everyone. They tend to over promise and stretch themselves thin, all with good intention but usually with disastrous results.

Heart-based magical girls are full of love but also have a sensitive soul that needs shielding from the toughness of the outside world. Remember to take care of yourself and give yourself the same amount of care and grace that you give to others. You can't be everything to everyone, so don't shy away from setting firm boundaries. It may be uncomfortable to advocate for yourself, but the people around you who love you want nothing more than to see you content and at peace.

Magical beings with heart powers: Sailor Moon (*Sailor Moon*), Steven Universe *(Steven Universe)*, Kiki (*Kiki's Delivery Service*), Layla (*Winx Club*), Naomi Osaka, Wangari Maathai

MOSTLY B'S: If you answered mostly B's, your magical girl power lies in your **Intelligence**. Intelligent magical beings find joy in problem solving. They don't shy away from obstacles and instead revel in the challenge of figuring it all out. Magical beings with intelligent power types are moved by mystery and let their curiosity lead them to amazing places and new heights. However, taking the space and time you need to analyze a situation can make others feel like you're hesitating, distrusting, or not passionate enough. This is simply untrue. You're so passionate that you're willing to dedicate a great deal of time to figuring out the task or mission at hand. Remember that it's perfectly okay to take your time, and it's a gift to be able to view the world through your unique, magical lens. Be sure to give the people you care about a heads up when you're deep in thought. I know you may think you're burdening them with the weight of the information you hold, but your magical accomplices would benefit greatly from knowing you're simply processing and not being secretive or lacking passion. A little bit of communication goes a long, long way.

Magical girls with intelligent powers: Sailor Mercury (*Sailor Moon*), Ladybug (*Miraculous: Tales of Ladybug & Cat Noir*), Pearl (*Steven Universe*), Tecna (*Winx Club*), Kizzmekia Corbett, Mae Jemison

MOSTLY C'S: If you answered mostly C's, your magical girl power is in the **Passion** category. Passionate magical beings have strong ideals and will fight tooth and nail for what they believe in. Magical beings with passion powers don't hesitate to stand up for themselves or others when faced with things like discrimination, inequality, and bullying. They empower others to advocate for themselves and stand up for what's right, always. Be careful though, your passion can sometimes grow into a raging fire that blinds you from seeing other points of view, so remain mindful and be open to hearing other people out. Not everyone holds a passionate flame that burns as bright as yours, so you can feel lonely at times, but remember you're incredible and you make quite the difference in people's lives. Many major world changes would not have been possible without powerful and passionate magical beings like you.

Magical girls with passion powers: Sailor Jupiter (*Sailor Moon*), Bloom (*Winx Club*), Michelle Obama, Malala Yousafzai, Mari Copeny

MOSTLY D'S: If you answered mostly D's, your magical girl power falls under the **Strength** category. Strong magical beings can fall down one hundred times, but they always bounce back stronger than ever! But don't confuse strength with rigidness. A strong magical being's true power lies in being flexible and changing course when things get tricky. Strong magical beings have the tenacity to take on any monster. Being strong doesn't mean you lack softness, either. Often, the strongest magical beings have the kindest hearts. They've had to build thicker skin as a response to the hardships of life.

When it comes to group dynamics, you often rush to take charge, but not everyone is used to the authority you hold. Remember to be patient, listen to others, and use their points of view to inspire the team's next steps. You're an amazing leader, and any team is lucky to have you!

Magical beings with strength powers: Garnet (*Steven Universe*), Sailor Mars (*Sailor Moon*), Serena Williams, Sha'Carri Richardson, Oprah Winfrey

MOSTLY E'S: If you answered mostly E's, your magical girl power falls under the **Creativity** category. Creative magical beings are chameleons in the best way. Whether it's through storytelling, art, fashion, or music, a creative magical girl knows how to captivate their audience. Creative magical beings can't be pinned down in one place for too long. They love a change in scenery and traveling to new, unexplored places—anything to inspire them and add some sparkle to their lives and art. You yearn to express yourself and can feel stifled when life's monotony catches up to you. But remember, you're a creative genius and there are always ways to shake things up while you wait for more adventure. Don't neglect your friends and family in your creative pursuits. Check in with your loved ones. They may even inspire your next creation!

Magical beings with creative powers: Creamy Mami (*Creamy Mami*), Musa (*Winx Club*), Doja Cat, Telfar Clemens, Amy Sherald, Toni Morrison

Congratulations, you've officially taken and passed the MGII and saved yourself years of tedious reflection and discovery. Go you! If you're tied between two categories, that's okay and perfectly normal. Your power can shift and change, or even combine into something amazing that's unique to you. But for the purpose of this exercise, follow your heart and pick the one that speaks the most to who you are in this moment. There's power in the pen, so grab one and write down your magical girl power in the space below:

_____

With this power, you're one step closer to becoming a magical girl. Don't you feel your inner magic glowing and growing already?

By now you may be wondering what makes me so qualified to be your temporary magical familiar, or how I've gained the knowledge to create such a test. Or maybe you're curious to know where my power lies. Lucky for you dear, sweet reader, I'm more than willing to share my lengthy journey of inner-magic discovery. Be warned, there are many twists, turns, and battles with inner monsters ahead. If that's not your thing, skip to Chapter Three. If it is, you're in for an epic tale of Myspace pages, corporate mess-ups, and a blossoming inner magic.

TWO

MY MAGICAL GIRL ORIGINS

In order for you to understand my magical girl journey, I've got to start at the very beginning. Growing up, I kept to myself, kept my mouth shut, and lived in fantasy worlds I created in my head. Because I spent so much time living in self-imposed obscurity, I didn't have many friends, but I didn't mind because I could always get lost in a story. During the week I'd escape into book after book, and on the weekends, Saturday morning cartoons like *Sailor Moon* brought fantasy worlds to life on my screen. Because of my love for fictional existences, English was my favorite subject, and I lived for the times we'd be assigned to write short stories for class. I'd craft bite-sized tales of ghost families, magical curses, and dystopian futures that I could slip into via daydreams when the real world's grayness got too heavy.

In high school, my passion for story telling eventually spilled onto the world wide web. At the time, social media networks were growing in popularity, and my entire class was making profile after profile and adding each other to multiple friends lists. It didn't matter if we were friends in real life, on the internet the rules of comradery were a bit looser and as long as you knew of someone, they'd be instantly "friended." After trying out a few online communities, I eventually settled on Myspace—the land of glitter text and top eight friends. I was thrilled to have a new outlet of expression outside of my fantasy stories and felt strangely safe in my little virtual world. Just like in my daydreams the internet was a place detached from reality, so I didn't feel compelled to disappear there. I finally had a platform!

After school I'd run home, and excitedly log onto Myspace to write about my teenaged thoughts and dreams. Sharing with my classmates on Myspace was like standing in the middle of Times Square, whispering a speech to busy passersby during rush hour. No one was interested in what I had to say, and understandably so, because in real life I wasn't very interesting. After all, I was deliberately disappearing at school like Sue Storm—The Fantastic Four's Invisible Woman. I eventually abandoned the barren land of Myspace and secretly ventured off to a new, relatively untraveled path—blogging.

I dedicated my first blog, *I Heart That*, to sharing all the whimsical, magical things I loved. Through my blogging escapades, I befriended an eclectic cast of online characters. There was the creative young woman with poetic thoughts who later became a screenwriter, an eclectic fashionista experimenting with her outfits, and a young, sometimes overly confident man who wrote about pop culture and social commentary.

Our comment sections became community gathering spaces, where I suddenly had dozens of people who genuinely cared about what I had to say. Online I transformed into a shinier, more magical version of myself. But in reality, I was hunched over my dad's desktop computer, clicking and clacking my thoughts on his keyboard in the dark. I kept my eyes on the screen and my ears tuned to hear the jingling of his keys in the front door, a signal he was home from work and my cue to hide my secret, magical identity.

My secret double life went on for years. Creating, writing, and sharing online was my passion, and I didn't care if I made a single red cent from my endeavors. In my real life, though, I was a bit embarrassed about my virtual hobby. I didn't know anyone else with a blog, and sharing anything that could potentially draw attention to myself wasn't part of my vanishing act. What I was unaware of at the time, though, was what I perceived as online oversharing and strange escapism was actually an unrefined creative gift. It wasn't until I paired that gift with the power of Heart that I really saw my world transform around me.

> **❝ Don't let fear of judgment drive you into the shadows, magical being! Embrace what makes you unique and step into your light. ❞**

After graduating high school, I retired my faithful blog. She served me well, but I was ready to shed my secret identity and make waves offline. I yearned for friends, real ones, like the Sailor Senshi I'd seen on television growing up. I wanted my very own transformation sequence and to experience all that life had to offer outside of my digital safe space. Because of my knack for disappearing and my small window of life experiences, teen makeover movies served as the inspiration for my evolution. Yeah, I know. Think Mia from *The Princess Diaries* or Cady from *Mean Girls*.

I sold my dull, childish clothing and all of my precious books to shed my nerdy, invisible skin. I probably made all of $80 for a pretty sizable collection which, upon reflecting, was definitely a rip-off but enough to pay for a brand new do. Armed with my stack of cash and a printed photo of Rihanna's edgy pixie cut, I made my way to the hair salon.

The hairdresser permed, washed, and dried my hair then snipped and snipped for what felt like an eternity. My hands shook in anticipation as she handed me a mirror to inspect her handiwork. I thought she'd whip my chair around and I'd emerge from a shower of light, looking as beautiful and otherworldly as the magical girls I'd always admired on TV. At the very least I thought I'd look somewhat like Rihanna. Of course, I was wrong. When I saw my reflection, it took everything in me not to scream. On my head was what loosely resembled Rihanna's fierce cut, except my hair was alarmingly stiff. Like I was wearing a hair-shaped helmet. The style didn't fit my baby face at all, and I felt so unlike myself. I quickly looked away from the mirror she'd handed me.

"Yay, I love it!" I lied through a strained smile, then handed her my cash and went through life with a hairstyle that was totally misaligned with who I was.

That salon experience would be the perfect analogy for my first year of college. I did everything to try to fit in, continually fighting against my innermost magical self.

I wore clothing I didn't love, pretended to like music I didn't care for, and tried morphing myself into someone I wasn't so I could befriend every single person I met. Long story short, it didn't work. When I finally grew tired of pretending, I stepped away from my peers and turned toward the internet, my safe space, once again.

Eventually, my secret online identity seeped into the real world, and my cover was blown. At first, I was embarrassed, but once everyone knew of my virtual life, what more was there to hide? I finally felt comfortable enough to experiment with my magical girl fashion in real life. I'd wear huge curly wigs, retro red lipstick, sickeningly girly dresses, and gaudy vintage jewelry. One day I wore a black suit with cascading gold chains and shiny Oxfords...to pottery class. Needless to say, I was bullied. However, looking back, I applaud myself for continuing to lay down my facade and creatively express myself, even in the face of ridicule. I didn't know it at the time, but I was slowly blossoming into my most magical form.

MAGICAL GIRL INTERMISSION

It's time to interrupt our regularly scheduled program to discuss embracing your passions. Many magical girls are reluctant to step into their power. Usagi cried. Marinette rejected her Miraculous. And I hid my power behind my secret online identity.

Now, I make a living doing those very things that I hid away from the people I knew, and the pre-med goals I had when I entered college faded long ago. I can't imagine how life would be if I continued to ignore my passions. I certainly wouldn't be writing this book!

What inner calling are you ignoring? What parts of yourself are you afraid to fully embrace? Contrary to popular belief, not every passion needs to be monetized. You don't even need to be good at it by society's standards. It just needs to be something you love.

Regardless of whether you make your passion your career or not, if you suppress the things that make you happy, you'll be uncomfortably bursting at the seams with untapped magic. Don't hide your light! Do what you love with a powerful passion and sense of joy. Live your life out loud, and the magic will surely hear your calls and find you.

 Life humbled me real quick when I graduated and left Kansas for Texas, only to anxiously and awkwardly fumble through job interviews while sleeping on a friend's couch.

 After a few months, I landed a marketing job at a hunting and boating company, and I had neither hunted nor boated in my life. Yet I was tasked with creating campaigns to attract camouflaged hunters to our website. I hated it.

Months went by and I trudged through my job duties as my inner glow waned and dulled. I was stuck in another gray place where I wasn't allowed to express my true self. Despite my unhappiness I still tried to be extra friendly and chat with my coworkers, but in return I was reprimanded for the way I dressed and belittled during meetings. When I showed my manager one of my business ideas, he asked me, "Who would buy that from you?" and that's when I knew I had to escape. After a few months, I quit my job and tried making a name for myself in the world of freelance marketing instead.

> **❝ Stifling your magic can lead you into dull, gray places where you feel you don't fit in. Don't settle for that. Branch out and let your inner power lead you to the places you belong. ❞**

Unfortunately, life continued kicking my butt. My time as a freelance social media marketer was both exciting and enlightening but also extremely draining. I lacked experience, wasn't fully aware of how much work I'd gotten myself into, and ended up just as underpaid, overwhelmed, and unhappy as I was at my job—and it was all my own doing. My poor clients saw my quality of work decline as my stress levels shot through the roof. My creative gift was waning by the day, and I struggled to juggle all of my self-imposed tasks and pay bills at the same time. I took on odd jobs that sucked the life out of me and made financial mistakes that sucked the money out of my bank account. And just when that last bit of light nearly faded from my spirit, I had an idea.

MAGICAL GIRL INTERMISSION

It's time to interrupt our regularly scheduled program to discuss making money as a grown-up magical being. In the popular web series *Bee and PuppyCat*, Bee is a magical woman in her twenties just trying to get by. She takes on low-paying jobs here and there but can't seem to stay employed long enough to regularly pay her bills. Yeah, I can definitely relate.

Luckily for Bee, a cat-like puppy familiar named PuppyCat falls from the sky and enlists her to take on mysterious odd jobs doled out by a space computer named TempBot. TempBot sends them to different dimensions, where they complete tasks in exchange for cold, hard cash.

Bee's plight isn't an uncommon one. When magical girls grow up, they still have to pay the bills, after all.

While I was living broke in Texas, I took on many odd jobs myself. While they were stressful, they paid the bills and taught me more about my most magical self. Working at a vintage shop fueled my interest in unique fashion. The customers were so eclectic, and I enjoyed playing personal shopper and making people feel more magical than when they first stepped in.

Working at a CPR training company, I was given free rein to design the company logo and website, and it really put my creativity to the test. It was also nice knowing I was helping save lives in my own tiny way.

I share all this to say, we all go through our struggles. Even fictional magical girls hustle to pay the bills from time to time! And as much as it sucked there was a bit of a silver lining. A friend once told me jobs are like colleges that pay you. You can use them as crash courses to learn whatever you need to on the job. While college left me with a mountain of debt, a job paid my rent every month. Reframing the way I saw work definitely helped me when I needed the motivation to keep pushing. Try looking past the drudgery and seeing every odd job as an opportunity to learn more about yourself and your magic. Then, once you can quit...make a mad dash to more magical pastures!

One day I took fifty dollars to my local Hobby Lobby, bought a pack of headbands and hot glue, then crafted like my life depended on it. I created crowns of sunflowers, pom poms, orchids, and roses. I styled the crowns on myself, and eventually, on my friends, in hyperfeminine shoots taken with my trusty, old DSLR camera. Each shoot told a magical story through photos taken in gardens, at parks, and backyards. I had a mission in mind: create an online space where dreamy, feminine, and quirky aesthetics could exist on Black bodies, where I could honor God with my talents, and where I could water that creative seed that was clinging onto my spirit for dear life. That's when I created my e-commerce business, Adorned by Chi, and things finally took a turn for the better.

Adorned by Chi started out as a simple site to sell my handmade wares and showcase Black women being whimsical and cute. With each order, I'd include a "love note" encouraging customers to be kind to themselves, reminding them that they were worthy of love, and letting them know they mattered in this world. These were all the things I needed to hear myself, and I wanted to reach people so they never felt as down as I did. With each pink package I sent out the door, I felt my magical seed growing and sprouting. The creativity and skill I'd been building through my online escapades were amplified by the power of my Heart and people caught on quickly. I found a girl gang of other small business owners, and we'd support and uplift one another. I managed to get my crowns in the hands of Chloe x Halle and worn by Jhene Aiko. True story!

Within two years, I grew my business from handmade flower crowns to girly, emotionally expressive tees celebrating my nerdy, magical girl identity and my business rapidly evolved into earning six-figure sales.

In 2018, I finally tapped into my passion for storytelling, put pen to paper, and crafted a magical girl–inspired tale with five Nigerian characters—Adaeze, Kaira,

Emeka, Gogo, and Kelechi—each with their own unique struggles and power bestowed by Igbo goddesses, who must fight an apocalyptic beast and save humanity. I ended up raising $18,000 via Kickstarter to bring the fictional world of Adorned by Chi to life, and I watched as my customers turned into readers, excited to learn more about the tale I was weaving.

Even more important than the sales, the collaborations, or the fundraising was my discovery of my magic. No, I wasn't whisked away to a faraway land by some mysterious creature. I didn't stumble upon an ancient magical artifact. I simply opened my heart to the everyday magic that was there all along. As more and more people joined my community of customers, readers, and supporters, I finally chipped away at the wall that I'd erected over the years to protect my hesitant heart. I was amazed and shocked by the support. I didn't think I deserved it, until finally I started to believe those love notes I'd sent out could apply to me as well. And just like in *The Wizard of Oz*, my gray world finally melted away into a technicolor land of enchantment. I finally found a way to live my stories and daydreams out loud.

> **Life is hard, and so many challenges will pop up on your journey through it. But keep going. Keep pushing through and trying new things. Eventually you'll discover that magic in the mundane.**

It took me as long as a decade to define my Heart power, and I discover new facets of my magic every day. Your power category isn't some static label to slap on yourself. It's guidance to lead you toward your true destiny. Are you an intelligent magical being with an interest in gardening? You can use your inquisitive nature and your passion to care for an arsenal of potted plants to teach your friends and family how to do the same. A passionate magical being with an interest in comic books? You can collect comic books to donate to children in need. My power was a desire to help others through my passion for online storytelling. When you combine your power with your passion, you're bound to make magic.

Now that you know my story, think about your own life's journey. What are you passionate about? What sets your heart aflutter? What could you enthusiastically go on and on about? Jot down your dreams in the space below.

Example: I'm passionate about helping young women feel seen and understood. I'm passionate about creating a safe space in my community. I'm passionate about helping those who need it.

_____

_____

_____

How can you combine your magical power with your passion?

Example: I can use my intelligence powers to plan and execute a community gathering, with events and speakers meant to empower young women.

_____

_____

_____

Knowing where your power lies is only a small part of the magical girl experience. Yes, it's true that we all hold power, but to become the best magical being you can be, you also have to train and maintain your power. It's just like a muscle. You have to strengthen those magical muscles through inner work, outer work and, of course, by reading this guide. The next few chapters will walk you through the process of embracing your brand-new magical girl identity.

THREE
CHOOSE YOUR NAME

What's in a name? Well, when you're a magical girl—everything! Once Usagi Tsukino declares "Moon prism power, makeup!" the reincarnated moon princess transforms into Sailor Moon—the Pretty Guardian of Love and Justice. Then there's Yū Morisawa, a young girl granted a magical wand that allows her to transform into a magical pop sensation. She names herself Creamy Mami, inspired by her family's Creamy Crepe shop. These names hold meaning to each magical girl and directly relate to their background, personality, power, or destiny.

Magical girl names are hardly ever simple. Of course, there are exceptions to the rule, but for the most part they're as magical, feminine, and decorated as the costumes our heroes wear after emerging from their dazzling transformation sequences. I love my name. But charging into battle declaring "Jacque's here!" doesn't elicit the same feelings as a name like Sparkly Plantain Warrior, for example. That name makes you want to know more. It sends off a warning signal that I have arrived and I've got the power of love, friendship and, apparently, plantains by my side.

> ❝When it comes to your name, only you can come up with something powerful enough to represent your magical being!❞

When I finally embraced my inner Heart power, I chose Adorned by Chi as the magical moniker for my business. To "adorn" something means to "make [that something] more beautiful," and "Chi" essentially means God, or your inner spirit, in my Nigerian Igbo language. I was moved to let my customers know they were made beautiful by a higher power. I also think "Adorned by Chi!" makes a pretty great magical girl battle cry. Combining my culture with my faith made for the perfect representation of who I was. And, with this name, I proudly charged into the world, shouting out about empathy, softness, representation, and magical girls until "Adorned by Chi" and the world I built around that name became synonymous with those terms.

The Magical Girl Identifier Index is a great tool for defining your power type, but when it comes to your name, only you can come up with something powerful enough to represent the totality of your magical being. While I can't choose a name for you, I can guide you in the right direction. The next few questions will serve as a guide to help inspire your magical girl moniker. Grab your trusty pen and write your answers in below. As always, let your inner magic guide you!

MAGICAL GIRL NAME GENERATOR QUESTIONNAIRE

Refer to the last chapter. What is your magical girl power category?

Example: My magical girl power is Heart.

What message do you want to declare to the world?

Example: I want to become a champion for diversity and inclusion in media.

_____

_____

What things in your life matter most to you?

Example: My faith, my career, my peace of mind.

_____

Who in your life matters most to you?

Example: My mother, my brother, my sister, my children.

_____

If you could only wear one color for the rest of eternity, which would you choose?

Example: Pink!

_____

What's one dish you could eat every day for the rest of your life?

Example: Plantain.

_____

What hobbies do you do in your spare time?

Example: Dancing, playing video games, and collecting wine glasses.

_____

_____

What are three words a friend would use to describe your personality?

Example: Goofy, introspective, creative.

_____

What are some of your favorite words?

Example: Magical, poofy, dire, indeed.

_____

When you were younger, what did you want to be when you grew up?

Example: A mad scientist.

_____

What's your dream career?

Example: A writer.

_____

Which of these words speaks to you the most? Choose only two.

Sparkly, Magical, Shiny, Cute, Princess, Star, Goddess, Angel, Heavenly, Creamy, Queen, Bright, Mystical, Glitter,

Revolutionary, Shimmering, Sailor, Pretty, Lyrical, Honey, Warrior, Star, Miraculous, Noir

_____

_____

Need a little more inspiration? Here are some names that came to mind from our examples:

- Revolutionary Shiny Scientist!
- Angel Scribe!
- Pink Lyrical Honey!
- Miraculous Star Sister
- Shimmering Wine Goddess

Now, study your answers above and pull out two to three words that speak to you, then arrange them however you'd like in the space below.

_____

Read what you've written out loud. This is your magical girl moniker. This name represents who you are, who you see yourself as, and how the world will receive you. Carry it with pride, and as you charge into battle, yell it out so your enemies can hear you coming and start shaking in their no-good, unfashionable boots!

With this name, you're nearly ready for your brand-new magical life. But wait! Before you go printing off name tags and business cards with your new moniker, you must take hold of your weapon.

FOUR
CHOOSE YOUR WEAPON

> **"** *The only limit to your magical weaponry is the depths of your imagination.* **"**

A magical girl's weapon is so important! While your magic is always brewing within, it's drawn out and harnessed through your weapon of choice. In the real world, we get the power of choice when it comes to our weaponry, but fictional magical girls don't often get that luxury. Instead, their weapons are often handpicked and gifted to them by a mythical being of some sort, or passed down like an heirloom. When discussing weapons, I think it's also important to note that magical girls aren't violent. Okay, they can be, but for the purposes of this guidebook, we're focusing on the ones who simply zap their adversaries into another dimension or rid them of whatever evil force has taken over their bodies. Real-life magical beings don't cause harm to people. What I describe as "weapons" are just tools to concentrate and redistribute your inner power out into the world.

In the Disney Channel series *Star vs. the Forces of Evil*, Star Butterfly is a reckless interdimensional princess with a penchant for punching monsters in the face. On her fourteenth birthday she's given her family's Royal Magic Wand and entrusted with the task of mastering its magic. As soon as Star touches the wand it transforms into a fierce purple scepter with a gold star, wings, and a crown on top—the perfect representation of Star's being. With her newfound power, she swiftly, and accidentally, sets fire to the kingdom and she's sent to Earth to train in a "safer environment." It's not long before a creature named Ludo catches wind of the wand's location and the weekly monster-battling adventures begin.

Another magical girl with a standout weapon? Creamy Mami! In the classic '80s magical girl series, Yū Morisawa is given a magical heart-shaped wand... by a space alien. The alien grants her powers for one year, and Yū wastes no time getting acquainted with her newfound magic. She quickly transforms into a lilac-haired teen and makes a name for herself in the world of music! When she's thrust into the spotlight, she realizes she needs a little help, and her wand shapeshifts into a magical microphone, which grants her the gift of song.

Most magical girl weapons are similar to Star's or Creamy Mami's. Heroes take hold of star-shaped staffs, heart-shaped compacts, or centuries-old magical alien wands, but here in the real world, there's actually a multitude of magical tools all around you. These are the weapons that you unknowingly wield every day to fight the tedium of life. That journal you pour your heart into? The cell phone that connects you to your loved ones? That mixing spoon you use to bake cookies when you're feeling a little down? There's power in all of these things! Even this book can serve as your weapon. From mystical microphones that can sing your foes to sleep to enchanted pens that can craft a tale that suddenly comes to life, the only limit to your weaponry is the depths of your imagination.

It's time to interrupt our regularly scheduled program to discuss finding bits of magic in the world around you. No, we can't grab hold of a magic wand that's been crafted in another dimension, but we can become more mindful of the little things around us that bring us joy.

Start paying attention to the moments during the day that make you smile. It could be those seconds after you've sprayed your favorite perfume. Or maybe the jolt of excitement you feel when your phone dings and you see a text from a friend you cherish. Those are magical moments, nestled in the mundaneness of everyday life. Magic in the real world is illusive. It doesn't go searching for a host to send off on a life-threatening mission. It hides away, quietly peeking out from time to time, waiting for us to slow down and notice.

When you catch glimpses of that magic, document it. Grab a journal and write out how you felt in those moments. Over time, you'll have a collection of good feelings and magical memories to return to when you're not feeling your best. There is truly magic to be found all around us.

DISCOVERING MY MAGICAL WEAPON

My magical girl weapon of choice is a pen. As soon as my tiny hands could hold a pencil, I was spinning magical tales. My earliest memory of my pen-wielding power was in elementary school, when we were tasked with creating our very own books. Everyone else wrote and illustrated their stories during our allotted times throughout the day, but my story was far too long and way too epic to be written in the short amount of time they gave us. I needed to tell the entire story of the Johnsons—a family that gains powers after an explosion during a cookie factory tour. I couldn't rest until my work was complete. I even brought my work home with me and stayed inside while my classmates played four-square during recess. At long last, I finished my story, barely making the deadline.

Later, my school held a ceremony where each student received a copy of our hardcover book. Holding that book in my hand, with its crayon-colored illustrations, shook me to my core. I was an author, and the Johnson family mutating after that unfortunate cookie factory accident set my world ablaze with a newfound passion. Since then, I've used my trusty pen to create worlds, like Adorned by Chi, write about feelings, and connect with people across the world through stories. With my pen, I've created this guide! And I continue to make magic through my creativity.

Now that you know my chosen weapon, let's get familiar with other potential weapons.

pen

perfume bottles

powder brush

notebook

MAGICAL WEAPON TYPES

PENS: Magical beings who call upon the power of the pen are mighty warriors with the ability to warp reality in whatever way they choose. They can create entire universes with the single stroke of their weapon. Story lines and plots are at their mercy, and they can move masses with their passionate prose.

Tomi Adeyemi is a magical girl who wields the power of her reality-shaping pen.

MICROPHONE: Microphones are the weapon of choice for magical beings with a message worthy of amplifying into the universe. Be it through beautiful music or sharing messages of social justice, mic-wielding magical girls are powerful beyond measure.

Beyoncé Knowles-Carter and Amanda Gorman are the perfect models of magical girls brandishing their microphones to spread empowering messages across the globe.

MAKEUP BRUSH: Magical beings who wield makeup brushes are masters of creativity and shape shifting. Faces become a canvas, and their artwork transforms people into walking, talking works of art.

Beauty gurus Jackie Aina and Nyma Tang are excellent examples of what a magical girl can do when wielding a makeup brush.

PAINTBRUSH: Magical beings who charge into battle with the power of the paintbrush are able to harness their creativity to transform the world around them. In the presence of a paint-brush-wielding magical girl, that dullness we've all felt at some point in our lives melts away into a colorful world of infinite possibilities.

Bisa Butler is a great example of a magical girl using her paintbrush to change the world.

WRISTWATCH: I know what you're thinking: "A wristwatch, really?" But magical beings who fight life's challenges with the support of time management and an appreciation of every passing second are super powerful! They get a whole lot of battling done in a little bit of time.

Business-savvy beauty mogul Cashmere Nicole used her power of time management to build a super-sweet, multi-million-dollar brand.

CELL PHONE: This is similar to Sailor Mercury's mini-supercomputer. Intelligent magical beings use their cell phones to analyze the world around them and quell their curiosity. Sometimes this is with a quick Google search, and other times it's hours and hours of research to feed their need for knowledge.

Raven the Science Maven is a super-smart magical girl spreading her message of diversity in STEM across the world using her supercomputer.

MIXING SPOON: Creative magical beings with a love for tasty treats choose to fight with cooking utensils! A magical mixing spoon takes simple ingredients and mixes them into delectable dishes that bring their enemies to their knees.

Tabitha Brown is a creative magical girl who fights conflict and setbacks with her culinary prowess.

ATHLETIC SHOES: Magical girls who fight with super-powered running shoes grab life by the horns and run over their adversaries—with love, of course.

Tennis superstar Serena Williams and track star Caster Semenya both train hard and dash past their competition with sparkly athletic shoes.

TROWEL: Magical beings with green thumbs use their trowels to grow illustrious floral gardens and beautiful plants that would bring any toxic villain to their knees.

Danny Clarke is a horticulturist who designs magical gardens and fights the monotony of life with his trusty trowel.

STETHOSCOPE: Stethoscope-wielding magical beings are truly the heartbeat of the universe. They're healers with a passion for ridding the world of disease and despair.

Any magical being in the field of healthcare has a stethoscope in their arsenal of magical weapons.

Remember, these aren't the only magical girl weapons to choose from but should inspire you while you decide which object will become your powerful scepter of love and justice. After you've given it some thought, use the space below to draw your shiny new weapon. Be as creative as you can and incorporate elements into the design that matter to you—like Star and her purple star-embellished wand, or Creamy Mami and her pastel-colored microphone.

Would you look at that. It's so beautiful I could cry! You've taken another huge step toward becoming a bona fide magical being. Now that you've identified your magical girl power, given yourself a unique and purpose-filled name, and donned your weapon of choice, you need someone, or something, to guide you and help you harness that inner power. You need a magical familiar.

FIVE
FINDING YOUR FAMILIAR

Every magical girl needs an uplifting and reliable companion by her side! Familiars are a staple, not only in magical girl anime, but across all magical worlds and universes. In *Revolutionary Girl Utena*, our main magical girl Anthy is accompanied by an adorable monkey named Chu-Chu. Honestly, he doesn't do much. But his presence serves as comedic relief, and sometimes that's enough. In *Sailor Moon*, Usagi has the wise and whip-smart black cat Luna to guide her. And in *Cardcaptor Sakura*, Sakura's mentor is a tiny, winged lion cub creature named Kero. These mystical creatures are there to show our magical girls the ropes, teach them about their powers, and offer them tough love from time to time. Or, in the case of Luna, all the time. Sometimes familiars talk, sometimes they don't, but their magical girl always understands them—even if no one else does. In the world of magical girls your familiar finds you; you don't get to choose them. But in the real world it's not so common for a furry creature to hop up to you and tell you that you have magical powers. Instead, we have a little more freedom and can choose our own familiar.

Before we dive into my journey of finding my familiar, let's uncover yours! Similar to the five categories of magical girl powers, through my extensive research into the art of real-world magic, I've discovered there are five main categories of magical familiars: cats, puppies, bunnies, mythical creatures, and ambiguous creatures. Of course, as with all things, there are some outliers and exceptions to the rules. I know of magical beings with monkeys, wombats, mice, frogs, rock stars, and even Yakuza-esque pixies fighting beside them. While your familiar could be whatever you can imagine, my Familiar Discovery Tool will help you discover which of the five main categories fits your personality best. Answer each question as honestly as possible and let your inner power guide you.

FAMILIAR DISCOVERY TOOL QUESTIONS

Which of the following describes your personality best? You can only pick one option.

A. You always mean well but you're a bit clumsy and end up with your foot in your mouth often.

B. You've got a soft and sensitive soul, so you take a while to warm up to new people.

C. You've got a lot of amazing ideas, but you're hesitant to pull the trigger and take action.

D. You're curious about the world around you, and you're continually searching for deeper meaning beyond the surface.

E. You're highly motivated and a hard worker, but a bit forgetful. You need things like sticky notes and calendar alerts to keep you on track.

It's after five, and you're finally free. Which activity would you rather do to take your mind off work?

A. Winding down with a multistep skin care routine.

B. Spending time outside in nature.

C. Reading a new, inspiring book.

D. Watching an interesting, yet strange, documentary.

E. Watching an old favorite movie or TV show.

Your friends take you to a new restaurant. What do you order?

A. Something random you've never tried before.

B. You like what you like, so you order an old favorite.

C. You let your friends choose for you.

D. You tell the waiter to "surprise you."

E. You ask the waiter which dish is the most popular and pick that.

Which of the following would you like to improve on?

A. Becoming more focused and productive in general.

B. Getting out more and making new friends.

C. Having more courage to jump at new opportunities as they come.

D. Becoming more in tune with the world beyond the surface.

E. Gaining more direction in life. You need a purpose.

Which quote resonates with you?

A. "You must live for those that love you."

B. "No matter how much you change, please don't forget there are people who care for you."

C. "I think it's better to leave with decorum and great dignity."

D. "You will have all the strength you will need inside. And you have a future only you can create."

E. "What's done is done. We can't change what happens but can only move forward."

What do you usually do when faced with a difficult challenge?

A. You cry your eyes out!

B. You ask your friends for advice.

C. You question yourself and go through a lot of back and forth inner dialogue.

D. You meditate and try to find the answers within.

E. You put things off until you absolutely have to face them.

Which scenario best describes your dream life?

A. Living in a quaint and quiet cottage with a sprawling garden where you grow strawberries and peaches alongside your soulmate.

B. Living in a fast-paced futuristic city with super-interesting neighbors. There's never a dull moment!

C. Living in a huge house with your many loved ones. You're constantly surrounded by warmth and love.

D. Being swept away to a mysterious land filled with unicorns, dragons, and fairies. It's dangerous, but exciting.

E. Living in a simple home with many doors that lead to random universes—each with a problem that you feel you must solve.

What is your greatest fear?

A. Letting fear get in the way of your dreams.

B. Living a life without love.

C. Not reaching your full potential.

D. Living a mundane life.

E. Being forgotten.

ANSWER KEY

Now that you've completed the Familiar Discovery Tool, it's time to tally up. Let's see which familiar type will guide you through your magical journey.

MOSTLY A'S

If you answered mostly A's, your furry friend will be a cat-type. Fierce feline sidekicks bring spunk, wit, and wisdom to the table. Magical beings most drawn to cat types are usually in need of a level-headed companion to push them through their moments of self-doubt and balance out their emotions. Cat types are wise beyond their years, which says a lot because most are older than a millennium. You can never go wrong with a feline companion!

Examples of cat-type magical familiars: Luna and Artemis (*Sailor Moon*), Jiji (*Kiki's Delivery Service*)

MOSTLY B'S

If you answered mostly B's, your familiar will be a puppy-type. Puppy-type familiars are lovable, huggable, and extremely loyal. More reserved magical beings who want to tiptoe out of their shell from time to time do well with puppy types. Puppies love to be on the go and make new friends. But even as they socialize with others and bring them together, they always stay loyal to their day one magical girl.

Examples of puppy-type magical familiars: Latte (*Healin' Good Pretty Cure*), Puff (*Go! Princess Pretty Cure*), Pekorin (*KiraKira Pretty Cure a la Mode*)

MOSTLY C'S

If you answered mostly C's, you're best suited for a bunny-type familiar. Bunny-type sidekicks are quick to jump at any opportunity to defend their magical being. Having a companion that pushes you to take action is so important for a more hesitant magical being. A bunny familiar is bound to make you stronger and more confident in trusting your inner magic.

Examples of bunny-type magical familiars: Kiko (*Winx Club*), Milk (*Yes! Pretty Cure 5*)

MOSTLY D'S

If you answered mostly D's, you're inclined to attract the guidance of a mythical creature. Mythical creatures are other-worldly animals like dragons, fairies, and unicorns. They come with a wealth of magical knowledge. Inquisitive magical beings who yearn for more are drawn to the mystique of mythical creatures.

Examples of mythical creature–type magical familiars: Kero (*Cardcaptor Sakura*), Spike (*My Little Pony: Friendship Is Magic*), Primera (*Magic Knight Rayearth*)

MOSTLY E'S

If you answered mostly E's, then you're most magically aligned with an ambiguous creature. We don't know what they are, but they're cute and can recall almost anything you'd need to know in a pinch. Ambiguous creatures are highly intelligent and bring a lot of facts and figures to the table to assist their magical girl. Magical beings with a lot on their plate would do well with an ambiguous creature by their side.

Examples of ambiguous creature-type magical familiars: Tikki and Plagg (*Miraculous: Tales of Ladybug & Cat Noir*)

Now that you know what type of familiar your heart is drawn to, it's time to draw your own loyal sidekick. Grab a pen or pencil, and use the space below to sketch out and name the familiar of your dreams.

Oh my goodness. How cute! Your magical familiar is here to guide you through life's many ups and downs. If you ever need guidance when wielding your powers, you basically have a walking, talking, sometimes flying embodiment of a magical encyclopedia beside you at all times. Remember, besides a wealth of magical knowledge, familiars are just like us. They're flawed, they speak out of turn, and they also mess up. But the beautiful thing about having a familiar by your side is knowing they've got your back no matter what.

I've always loved cat-type familiars like Jiji, Luna, and Artemis, but as a magical girl on the shyer side of the spectrum, I've found myself drawn to puppy-type familiars who ease me out of my shell. My search for a familiar wasn't the most magical journey. There were definitely some twists and turns, but in the end, I found my furry companion Nala. If you're curious to know more about the search for my familiar, read on. If not, skip to the next chapter.

THE SEARCH FOR MY FAMILIAR

When I was a teenager with a brand-new driver's license, I decided to reward myself with a vanilla ice cream cone for surviving another day lurking in the shadows of high school. That cone was piled high with creamy, swirly goodness. Even though I'm lactose intolerant, I threw caution to the wind because I was determined to treat myself. Windows down, I let the wind whip through my microbraids as I drove around, music blasting, with a smile spread across my face. But my euphoria ended when I pulled up to my parents' driveway and stepped out of my car. That's when I saw a tiny, fluffy creature staring back at me.

I now know that I was staring down a Pomeranian, but at the time all I saw was a tiny, scary, hairy beast. The beast's tail wagged feverishly, and its little, pink tongue carelessly hung out of its mouth. We stared at each other for what felt like an eternity but was probably less than a second before I screamed at the top of my lungs. I turned and ran. The beast chased. I was certain I was on the verge of death and my short life flashed before my eyes. In a last-ditch effort to escape, I threw what was left of my perfect ice cream cone, and the miniature monster followed it. I darted back home, slammed the door behind me, and fell to my knees, holding back tears. I share all this to say, growing up I was never really into pets. But things have since changed.

MAGICAL GIRL INTERMISSION

It's time to interrupt our regularly scheduled program to discuss fear. Fear, as an emotion, serves its purpose as a warning signal for the body to let you know that danger's on the horizon. The downside is, you can become so hardwired to being afraid that fear is triggered even when there's no real threat at all. This idea of being hardwired in a state of fear is explored in the Cartoon Network series *Steven Universe Future*, which we will cover on page 134.

Before meeting my first familiar, I was deathly afraid of dogs. Didn't matter the breed, size, or temperament. If I saw a dog, I'd instinctually run off. And of course, the dog would chase, playfully, but I didn't know that. Over time, I've come to realize this was an irrational fear, and now I absolutely love dogs. When faced with fear, ask yourself if there's really an imminent threat to your safety. If not, there are ways to push back and overcome.

One way to push back is to gain an understanding of the thing you fear. Pull out your handy dandy phone and google the object of your fright to learn more about it. We tend to fear the unknown, but with a little understanding, you can shrink that towering fear monster into a tiny creature of curiosity.

For example, if what you fear is a person, reflect on why they may be behaving the way they are. You'd be surprised to learn that many "scary" people aren't scary at all, they're just hiding their hurt behind a towering wall. That doesn't justify any cruel behavior, but it can help you feel more empowered to stand up for yourself. Sometimes all it takes is seeing things from a different perspective to send fear running for the hills.

When the time came and I was ready to open my heart and my home to a new pet, I had a hard time finding a fit. I truly didn't think I'd ever be able to fill the tiny, dog-shaped hole in my soul. But one November afternoon, I followed my best friend Rachel to our nearest pet adoption center. She was in search of an athletic dog she could run with, and I tagged along because that's what friends do! There were so many lovable dogs at the shelter in need of a home, and many of them pulled at my heartstrings, but none of them felt like my perfect match.

After some time, my friend found her dream dog. As they opened his cage so we could interact with him, I looked over and saw what they called the "small dog area." That's when I noticed a tiny, long-haired Chihuahua in a dusty pink coat, with bandaged paws, cowering in the corner of her cage. Her name was Petal.

"Can I also see that one?" I asked, pointing to the terrified animal.

The volunteers pulled her out of the cage, but she refused to walk, so she was carried, coat and all, to the socialization area outside. As Petal stood in place, refusing to move, shivering from fear rather than the cold, I knew I had found my new familiar. I took her home that day and named her Nala.

Nala spent her first few days with me staring into my soul with her big black eyes from the safety of her little cage. She refused to go down any stairs, so whenever she needed to go potty, she was carried to and fro like the tiny princess she was. After some time, her dew claws healed and we could remove her bandages. That's when she started to inch out of her cage, both literally and figuratively.

Almost two years later, Nala and I are two peas in a pod. She trails me like a shadow and plops in front of me when she feels I need protecting—or when she wants to be petted. Because my monsters don't plague me as often as they used to, she's usually just there for the pets. I couldn't ask for a better magical girl familiar than Nala. She's loving, loyal, and loves naps and food just as much as I do. When I find myself disappearing, she pulls me out of the shadows and into the dog park, where I'm forced to interact with the world. We're truly a match made in magical girl heaven.

Now you know how my hunt for a familiar went down, and you've dreamt up one of your own. You're making so much progress! This is the point in our journey together where I hand off my baton as your temporary magical familiar. I've gotten you this far, but it takes a more powerful being than I to take you to new heights—your magical familiar! With your brave and loyal familiar by your side, you're almost ready to take on the world. Almost. No one person can face the menacing forces of the world on their own, even with the guidance of a familiar. You need a crew of equally powerful friends to really make magic happen!

SIX

YOUR MAGICAL GIRL GANG

Magical girls are nothing without their support system. Friendship and magic go hand in hand, after all. Would the ladies of Winx Club stand a chance against the Trix, episode after episode without leaning on one another? Nope! And would the Sailor Senshi be able to foil Queen Beryl's plans time and time again on their own? Absolutely not! No magical being is an island, and it truly takes a village, or a team of magical people, to come together and defeat the forces of evil.

Nothing is more powerful than the bonds of friendship. Each hero has a special connection with their comrades that intensifies the strength of their collective magic. This isn't exclusive to battling bad guys either. Magical beings support each other, offering love, guidance, and a helping hand both on and off the battlefield. As important as it is to surround yourself with other powerful peers, tracking down members of your magical crew is no easy task. Making meaningful connections as an adult is hard enough, let alone finding friends who are willing to costume up and fight monsters beside you.

So, now that I've stepped down as your magical familiar, I'm stepping up as a member of your magical girl gang. Even when this guide comes to a close, you'll always have a comrade in me, magical being. And while I'll always be here, it's still important to expand your ranks and open your heart to deep friendships and new connections. After all, when things get tough, it's your friends who will be there supporting you and backing you up!

MAGICAL GIRL INTERMISSION

It's time to interrupt our regularly scheduled program to discuss supporting friends through every season. In Season 2 of *Sailor Moon*, Ami (Sailor Mercury) gets the opportunity to follow her dreams and study medicine in Germany. Ami struggles with her decision as she's always wanted this, but she doesn't want to leave her friends behind. Although they're sad to see their friend go, the other Sailor Scouts are supportive and want what's best for Ami. If that means studying in Germany, well, they'll just have to be besties from afar.

When the girls don't show up at the airport to see her off, the mischievous Chibiusa tries her best to convince Ami that her friends don't care about her. However, Ami knows something's wrong, and she abandons her flight to find the Sailor Scouts. It turns out they've been attacked by an ice-themed adversary, and they're in major trouble! In the end, Ami saves her friends from danger and decides to stay and study medicine in Japan instead. When the other girls ask why she's returned, she says, "Friendship is just way more important." This episode perfectly illustrates the significance of friendship for magical girls.

Are they powerful on their own? Yes! But together, they're an unstoppable force.

It's amazing that Ami's friends put their own feelings aside and encouraged her to follow her dreams without guilting her into staying. This is what good, supportive friends do. And Ami's choice to stay made perfect sense. She didn't want to abandon the other Sailor Scouts when they needed her most. If she didn't show up to help them, they could've died. That's some serious stuff!

While being a supportive friend means you sometimes have to sacrifice your comfort to help one another, it doesn't have to mean outright abandoning your own dreams and major opportunities. It would've been nice to see Ami save the day and still get on that plane to make her dreams come true but, in the end, she isn't totally abandoning her dream of becoming a doctor. She's just staying put to protect her loved ones, and that's always admirable.

Whether you would've gotten on the plane to study medicine in Germany or stayed in Japan with your magical girl gang, the key to a magical friendship is wholeheartedly supporting your friends through every season and allowing them the space to do what's best for them. Good friends want their friends to achieve their own personal definition of happiness.

FINDING MY MAGICAL GIRL GANG

When it comes to friendship, although it's an important part of the magical girl experience, I admittedly haven't always been the best at cultivating close bonds with people. I definitely had a few friends growing up, and I'm so grateful for them, but as a disappearing artist who spent more time in my fictional worlds than with my peers, no one ever stuck. So, when I started college, I was on a mission to change that. I wanted my very own magical girl gang! I introduced myself to everyone, smiled all the time, and was so excited at the prospect of making new friends. As you've probably gathered from the stories I've told about college—things didn't exactly go as planned. However, I didn't leave school empty-handed. I emerged, wounded and scarred, but propped up by some of the most amazing friends I'm blessed to know. One of those amazing people is my best friend, Rachel. We met in chemistry class, and that's fitting because together we make one magical bond.

Until college I was a straight-A student, and academics were always a breeze for me. But not College Chemistry I. That class was a major pain. I went from a tiny school with classes that rarely exceeded twenty students to a huge, daunting lecture hall with more students crammed into one classroom than attended my entire high school. Not only was I overwhelmed by the sheer number of humans sitting in one class, but I was also taken aback by our professor. He was a brash, barrel-chested man who didn't seem to care whether we lived or died, let alone passed or failed his class. Every single one of his lectures was an exercise in patience, as it took everything in me to fight my daily urge to drop his class. But the best thing to come out of his torturous lectures was meeting my best friend.

I actually don't quite remember what sparked my friendship with Rachel. Maybe because I was deep in my mad dash to make friends; maybe we were both in desperate need of study buddies; or maybe it was divine intervention, and we were destined to make a connection. But I like to say it was all three! Soon we were hanging out every day, exploring our newfound adulthood and bonding over our shared experiences—Rachel as a young Haitian immigrant and me as a first generation Nigerian American. We also bonded over the fact that we both failed our chemistry finals. Badly. Along with Rachel, I met a special handful of people who remained my friends through the good, the bad, and the ugly. And things definitely got real, real ugly.

Because I didn't have much experience socializing, let alone maintaining friendships, I made many mistakes. I isolated myself, closed myself off when people got too close and, after being bullied, completely shut down. I even distanced myself from Rachel. I saw every friend and acquaintance as a vehicle for potential disappointment—a stark contrast from the friendly, smiley girl I'd started as the previous school year. I was nervous and lonely, but my behavior came off as cold, standoff-ish, and wishy-washy. It was during this time that I was also diagnosed with severe social anxiety.

In case you don't know, social anxiety is the irrational fear of social situations. Anything from giving a speech to meeting someone new can trigger anxiety attacks and racing thoughts. Social anxiety is also my personal adversary, draining me of my magical energy week after week. Because I'd spent so much time alone in the past, I didn't realize just how ferocious my anxiety was until I found myself surrounded by people in college. I also unfortunately developed an irrational fear of stepping foot on campus. I'd catch the bus to class as usual, but as it drew nearer to the campus my Anxiety Monster would punch me right in the gut. I'd step off of the bus with everyone else to look inconspicuous but, as they dispersed, I sat at the bus stop alone until the next bus came around to take me home.

This fear led to my spending days alone in my room. I lived off of hot fries and Arizona iced tea that I scavenged from my kitchen cabinets like a rat, because I didn't even want to risk running into my roommates. As you can imagine, a fear of campus resulted in my skipping classes and withdrawing from my community. This embarrassing period started my years-long battle with anxiety and many of my friendships were sacrificed in the process.

Luckily, those few special friends held on to me, even when I was willing to spiral into complete fear-induced reclusion. Rachel would drive hours to visit me when we lived in different cities. I had friends who would be up at 3 a.m. with me, talking through our feelings together. And others would physically drag me out of bed when I wanted to do nothing else but hide my magic from the world. I will forever be grateful for the friends who have loved me through all my issues, and I also will forever do the same.

MAGICAL GIRL INTERMISSION

It's time to interrupt our regularly scheduled program to discuss judging a book by its cover. When we're first introduced to Ami in *Sailor Moon*, she's the smartest girl in school, earning the highest mock exam scores in the entire country. Her fellow classmates whisper behind her back to Usagi, speculating that the quiet girl is full of herself because of her high IQ. At the same time, Usagi's feline companion Luna senses a strange energy around Ami and immediately suspects she is a monster.

Usagi bats away the judgment of Luna and her classmates and befriends Ami anyway. Her intuition serves her well as it turns out Ami isn't a narcissistic monster after all. She's just shy, misunderstood, and focused on her studies. She also happens to be Sailor Mercury, one of the guardians Usagi had been tasked with tracking down.

This parallels my experience with social anxiety. While I was really just shy and scared like Ami, I came off as a standoffish, plan-canceling monster. If it weren't for my friends who had the grace and patience of Usagi, I would have never eased out of my shell.

Sometimes the quiet people we judge have a whole world of magic hiding out in their minds. Embody the spirit of Usagi and try not to judge a book before you've read a single chapter.

With every hug, every catch-up call, and every crying session, my heart grew larger and my walls chipped away. My friends and I fought the Anxiety Monster together, and it's through the force of these friendships that I was able to take hold of my magical pen and confidently embrace my inner Heart power. Now, years later, Rachel and I are still attached at the hip. We live within walking distance from each other, and my familiar Nala spends the weekends with her "Aunt Rachel," giving her the same magical girl guidance she gives me.

> **Sometimes it's a fight to make and maintain friendships, but for a magical girl, it's always worth the battle!**

Friendships are so important, but just like our magic, they take work. Unlike other outlets that tend to pit feminine people against each other, magical girls encourage us to embrace our besties and be steadfast in friendship during the highest of highs and the lowest of lows. Even if, like me, you struggle with making friends, it's very possible to find your people. You just might have to do it in more creative ways than others.

So far, I've been on all sides of the friend spectrum, from a lone wolf to a social butterfly. Currently I'm enjoying a happy medium with a small group of low-maintenance close friends. Along the way, I've stumbled through many friendships, but I've succeeded at making real connections with a special few. Because I've tried my hand at making friends in every way possible and have lost them too, I can tell you how to make friends, what not to do, and how to continue stoking the magical flames of friendship.

HOW TO MAKE FRIENDS AS AN ADULT MAGICAL GIRL

In *Sailor Moon*, Makoto Kino is the new girl at Juban Public Middle School. Rumors swirl of her being a mean girl as her classmates judge her for her appearance. She's taller and stronger than the other kids, with an air of independence that they likely don't understand. While her peers avoid her, Usagi, enamored by Makoto's bravery and wowed by her exquisite rose earrings, brushes off the rumors, walks right up to her, and gets to know her for herself. They quickly bond over Usagi's love for food and Makoto's culinary prowess. Surprisingly, Makoto isn't the "tough girl" she's been assumed to be. She's sweet and sensitive and loves love. She also happens to be one of the inner Sailor Senshi—Sailor Jupiter. While not all of us are as bold and open-minded as Usagi, we can all learn something from her about making friends.

> *"Magical Girls know better than to judge a book by its cover. Forget rumors and stereotypes. Get to know people for who they are."*

SOCIAL MEDIA: When you're in school, meeting friends is as easy as sitting next to someone at the lunch table or failing chemistry finals together. As a full-fledged adult in the real world, it's a bit trickier than that, but spontaneous warm connections, like Usagi meeting Makoto, are still possible. One way to meet people in the real world is through shared interests. Luckily, in this age of social media, it's easier than ever to find people who are into the same things you are. I've been in Discord chats with fellow cartoon lovers, I've connected with other soft fashion enthusiasts via Facebook, and I met one of my closest friends through Pinterest. Yup, Pinterest— the only social network that makes it incredibly hard to be social. But during my blogging phase a super-cool girl noticed my pins, and her boyfriend at the time reached out on Twitter to let me know she liked my content.

The adoration was mutual, and we've been friends ever since!

NETWORKING: Another way to make friends is through the ones you already have. We all have a network of people, from besties to distant associates, and sometimes putting yourself out there and meeting people through events and gatherings like weddings and birthday parties can work wonders. I met another close friend of mine through a business-related event we were both invited to. Not much happened on the business end of things, but I'm so grateful to have had the chance to cross paths with a future friend. We related to each other through my nonstop embarrassing blunders over the course of what was meant to be a very serious weekend. Now we talk almost every day, and I can't imagine not having her in my life.

SHARED INTERESTS: Do you spend time at the gym? Are you thinking of signing up for crochet classes? Are wine-tasting tours your thing? By engaging in activities you already love, you can make new friends who come with a built-in shared hobby or interest. Unlike networking events, which can be a bit awkward, meeting friends through shared interests makes connecting much easier.

WORK: You can also make friends at work. Chances are you spend most of your time at work, so naturally you will start to break the ice and chitchat with your coworkers about more than job-related topics. Inviting a coworker to lunch is the easiest way to get to know them better. But be careful! You don't want your friendship to affect your working relationship, so while you're still coworkers, my advice is to not get too deep. The people you work with don't need to know your deepest darkest secrets just yet. They need you to turn in your reports and meet your deadlines so they can meet theirs. Divulging too much personal information at work can lead to some awkward situations or even a call from HR.

Meeting people is one thing, but the next hurdle is figuring out what to actually say to people you do meet. As an official state-certified awkward duck, I've often found myself struggling to start and maintain conversations—both online and in person. But after lots of trial and lots of error, I've kept a running mental list of some conversation starters that may make things a bit easier for you too.

CONVERSATION STARTERS

WHAT HAVE YOU BEEN WATCHING LATELY?: Conversations usually kick off with the question of "So, what do you do?" but I personally avoid directly asking about careers. Work can be stressful for many, and that question puts people in formal, button-up mode. Instead, I ask, "What have you been watching lately?" Then, as they describe the plot and why they either hate it or love it, it opens the door for you to ask more questions to keep the conversation rolling. It's even better when you find you've watched the same show, or even enjoy the same genres. You'd be surprised how many people I've bonded with over our love of *Sailor Moon*.

DO YOU LIKE PODCASTS? I'M TRYING TO FIND A NEW ONE TO LISTEN TO. ANY SUGGESTIONS?: People. Love. Podcasts. I can't explain why, or when this podcast revolution even happened, but know that it's true! Personally, I'm a sucker for a funny or informative podcast, and I'm always excited to share recommendations with new people I meet.

I LOVE YOUR SHOES/DRESS/BAG, WHERE'D YOU GET THEM FROM?: Just like Usagi and Makoto, I've been enamored by many magical beings over their amazing sense of fashion. I love people who dress outside the bounds of social norms, so I'm naturally drawn to stand-out pieces. Most are excited to share their hidden gem thrift stores, favorite little-known small business, or disclose that they got a major deal at the mall. From there, we swap shopping tips and DIY hacks.

DO YOU KNOW ANY GOOD FOOD SPOTS AROUND HERE?: Food is like the glue that bonds humanity together. There's nothing more universally adored than a delicious meal, and people love sharing their favorite underrated restaurants. Take it even further by asking them what you should order when you go, then sit back and watch their eyes light up as they describe their usual.

HOW DID YOU HEAR ABOUT THIS EVENT? HOW DO YOU KNOW THE HOST?: This is one of the easiest ways to kick off a conversation. The other person can tell whatever funny, kooky, or even straightforward story led them to crossing paths with you. If you both know the host, you can bond over shared memories, or if it's an event, like a business networking summit, you can share your individual journeys that brought you both together.

SHARE SOMETHING ABOUT YOURSELF: You don't always have to ask the questions—you can share something about yourself too. When it comes to the question of what to share, it can be anything really, but be sure to keep it light and fun. Bring up a new show you're excited about, a new restaurant you tried and loved, or even just a funny story you love to tell. It takes pressure off of the other person and gives them the chance to get to know you better as well.

SLIDE IN THE DMS WITH A FUNNY MEME: With connections made via social media it's a little easier to break the ice. Usually, you can see the kinds of things your future friend enjoys and engages with. If you have those interests in common, you can slide into their DMs with a funny meme about it. While I'm on the shyer side and rarely message people first, I always enjoy when people hit me up about things I truly love.

So, take the leap and get to sliding!

Now that you know some ways to slide in and connect with your potential future friends, here are a few things you should avoid.

WHAT NOT TO DO

CROSSING BOUNDARIES

When you instantly click with someone, it can be tempting to completely open up to them, but you should take things slow. While it's always magical meeting new people because of how different we all are, you should always consider and respect differences in boundaries.

I've had people shoot their friend-shot at me and completely scare me away by oversharing or expressing negativity right off the bat. I'm never one to shy away from talking about unpleasant feelings and below-surface-level topics. But as a low-maintenance friend and someone who's dealt with bad friend experiences, my fight-or-flight instincts immediately activate, and I hightail it out of there. On the flip side, I've also had my own instances of oversharing that resulted in awkward conversation and the cold shoulder. This isn't always the case for everyone. Some may open up faster than others, but because your future friend is a current stranger, it's always best to play it safe and move at a comfortable pace.

GOSSIPING

Humans gossip. It's part of our nature to discuss happenings in our community with our close friends, and I'm not so removed from reality to suggest you stop altogether. However, gossiping with a potential new friend doesn't reflect well on the messenger. Whenever my first interaction with someone includes talking negatively about a person I have yet to meet, I'll always leave the conversation feeling sympathy for the subject of the gossip and distrust for the person gossiping. And just like Usagi, I'm likely to befriend the person being dragged through the mud instead. Your first impression means so much, why waste it speaking unkindly about someone else?

TAKING THINGS PERSONALLY

Sometimes we shoot our friend-shot, and it just doesn't work. Try not to take it personally! Even with the help of prompts, tips, and shared interests, conversations can fall flat and feel awkward. But it doesn't mean that anything is wrong with you. Maybe the other person's tired, maybe they're stressed, maybe you're stressed, or maybe you just don't click. It happens, and it can feel like the end of the world in the moment, but trust me, it's fine. With all of our magical differences, it only makes sense that we won't always become fast friends after one conversation.

Personally, I've later befriended people who thought I was standoffish at first because I didn't respond to them the way they thought I would. But what they don't realize at the time is, as I've mentioned, I have severe anxiety and a fear of letting people down. I'll be hesitant for a long while, not because I'm uninterested, but because I'm nervous! There are also times where I just don't have the mental bandwidth to build new friendships. I share all that to say—sometimes, it's not you, it's them, and sometimes, friendship is just not in the cards. And that's okay too!

If you shoot your friend-shot and it ends up working out—congrats! Now you may be wondering, "What am I supposed to do with this new person?" Don't worry, I've got you covered. Just like how magical girls grow closer together with each battle, two strangers become closer friends through shared experiences. The only way to have shared experiences is to take initiative, and your approach depends on what kind of friendship you have. Along my journey, I've learned that no one style of friendship is better than the other, and how you build and maintain bonds is totally up to you. However, it's important to understand what each friend-style entails and the different triumphs and challenges that come with each one. But before we dive into that, it's time for the Magical Girl's Friendship Style Assessment!

This assessment is meant to tell you what kind of connection you're looking for, and how to strengthen your friendships no matter what style you gravitate toward most. As always, answer honestly and let your inner power guide you.

MAGICAL GIRL'S FRIENDSHIP STYLE ASSESSMENT

It's Friday night and you don't have any plans. Suddenly, your phone dings, and there's a text from a friend, inviting you to a party that starts in three hours. Besides your one friend, you don't know anyone else who'll be there. So you:

A. Happily accept the invitation! You were hoping someone would invite you to something, and you already have an outfit planned in your head.

B. Thank your friend for the invitation, but you've already curled up under a blanket with a queue of YouTube videos ready to go.

C. Call up your besties and ask if they'd like to go. You move as a unit or you don't make moves at all! If they say yes, you head to the party together.

D. Turn down the invite. All your closest friends are spread out in faraway places, and you don't want to go alone.

It's been a long day of fighting monsters. What's your go-to hangout spot for you and your magical friends?

A. The newest, coolest brunch spot in town. Bottomless mimosas sound like the perfect end to a long day of magical battles. You and all your friends show up, eat well, and laugh the afternoon away.

B. You usually head home and unwind on your own, but when you do decide to hang out, it's at a local arcade/bar hybrid. A barcade, if you will. There's less talking and more game playing.

C. You and your friends have an after-battle ritual of sorts. No matter the location, you all manage to come together week after week to share funny stories, reminisce over past battles, and bond over shared interests.

D. You hang out virtually. Discord chats, FaceTime, and Zoom are where it's at for you and your crew.

How often do you see your closest friends?

A. I'm with people almost every day. Close friend or not.

B. I see my friends monthly at most.

C. I'm with my besties every weekend.

D. My friends are pretty far away, so I see them when I can—even if it's as little as once a year. But we text often.

As a magical team, how do your friends' powers complement yours?

A. It doesn't matter. I could team up with anyone at any time!

B. We don't team up often, but when we do, our powers are used in tandem and perfectly in sync. Similar to the Crystal Gem fusions from *Steven Universe*.

C. Our powers are totally different, but with strategy and teamwork we save the day together time and time again. Like the Sailor Senshi.

D. Our powers are complementary, but we're rarely in the same location so we rely heavily on telecommunication—like magical communicator watches.

Which choice describes your current friend situation?

A. I know a bunch of people, and I'm always invited to different events.

B. I have a small number of friends that I see from time to time.

C. I have a tight-knit group of friends, and we do everything together.

D. I mostly communicate with my friends via text, chat, and DMs.

Which of these do you think you need to work on?

A. Slowing down and checking in on the people I care about.

B. Putting the phone down and going out into the world to experience things in real life.

C. Spending time getting to know myself. I struggle to answer the question "Who are you?"

D. Living in the here and now instead of thinking of the past or worrying about the future.

What would your friends say about you?

A. "Oh yeah, they're cool! They know everyone, and they're always in the mix."

B. "We don't see each other often, but when we do it's always a great time!"

C. "That's one of my besties! We're thick as thieves, and no monster could ever tear our group apart."

D. "Love them! We talk every day, even though we're far apart."

Your friend has a major crush on someone you know. What do you do?

A. Invite them to the same event and hope that some magic sparks between the two of them.

B. Give your friend advice but stay out of it. You don't want to meddle with their potential romance.

C. Throw them in the same group chat and hint at a romantic connection.

D. Tell your friend to slide in those DMs!

A friend of yours doesn't know about your secret, magical identity. They're starting to put the pieces together though, since you always mysteriously disappear when monsters are afoot. So you:

A. Ignore their prying and invite them to a party instead!

B. Tell them there's no way you of all people could be a magical girl. After all, you barely even text back!

C. You wonder if your friend is being mind-controlled by a bad guy. All your friends know about your secret identity!

D. You leave them on read while you think up an excuse.

ANSWER KEY

And just like that, you've completed the Magical Girl's Friendship Style Assessment! Time to tally up and see which friendship style suits your personality best.

MOSTLY A'S: If you answered mostly A's, your friendship style is social butterfly. Social butterflies love being in the mix. You know of everyone, and everyone knows of you, so fluttering from friend group to friend group is easy peasy. You get invited to all the best events, wait no, you get invited to all the events, and you're always the life of the party. Life is amazingly exciting, and there's never a dull moment for you! The best part about being a social butterfly is being the first in mind when people have opportunities and cool things to share.

Now, the challenge with having so many friends is you may find yourself spread thin and struggling to create deeper bonds with people. While it's fun to continually frolic through fields of new friends, don't forget to water your garden and tend to your close friends who care most about you. If you find yourself craving closer bonds with people, from time to time you can take your friends out on "dates" where you just connect one on one or in a smaller group. Remember, people create close bonds through emotional openness and shared experiences, and that takes care, time, and attention. And you can always turn down invitations when you're feeling worn out. No one will hold it against you!

TIP: *If you're not a social butterfly but you're friends with one and want to strengthen your bond, it's important to initiate one-on-one time with your popular pal. They may not realize you're yearning for more time with them, and a gentle reminder or occasional check-in can make all the difference. If they value you, they will definitely add you to their schedule.*

MOSTLY B'S: If you answered mostly B's, then your friendship style is low maintenance. Low-maintenance friends are the kind you see once in a blue moon, but every time you connect it's like no time passed at all. I have a number of low-maintenance relationships, and they're truly my favorite kinds of bonds. Days, months, and even years pass between the times we spend time together, but we don't hold it against each other. Instead, in the interim, we occasionally send each other memes and funny videos then we react with crying laughing emojis and smile to ourselves before going on about our day.

Low-maintenance connections don't work for everyone, though. Be mindful of your friends and how they may feel when you go ghost, or disappear. Be sure to communicate your friendship style with them so they don't feel slighted in those times you need your space.

TIP: *If you don't have a low-maintenance friendship style and find yourself feeling iced out by a friend who likes to lay low, it's important to communicate those feelings. This doesn't mean calling them out and blaming them. That will only get their defenses up and may confuse them if they aren't intentionally giving you the cold shoulder. Instead, let them know you miss their presence and want to spend some time with them. A true friend will receive the message well and talk things through with you. Now, this doesn't mean they'll suddenly step out of their comfort zone to step up to your expectations of friendship. But they'll let you know what works for them, and you can both take it from there.*

Also be mindful that many low-maintenance friends may be more introverted or anxious. As a socially anxious low-maintenance friend myself, sometimes I get overwhelmed and need time to isolate. I make sure to communicate this with the people around me so when I go ghost, they know it's nothing personal. If you find yourself needing some space, be sure to communicate it to your friends. People will often blame themselves when a connection starts feeling less warm, and it's only fair to give them a heads up and to answer honestly when asked.

MOSTLY C'S: If you answered mostly C's, then your friendship style is small and close-knit. Having a small group of go-to friends is great for sharing memories and new experiences together. In a smaller group, it's much easier to grow closer, so you always know who's got your back and who you can count on. Plus, taking vacations together is so much fun!

The one downside of a close-knit group is friend fatigue. When you're always around each other, there's more opportunity to get on each other's nerves. When frustrations are high, it only takes one bad experience to unravel years of friendship.

TIP: *To beat friend fatigue, I suggest spending time with other friends outside of your core group so you can shake things up from time to time. Also, having varied interests and hobbies to keep yourself busy is always a positive, and taking a bit of time apart when things get tense can help immensely. Absence makes the heart grow fonder, after all!*

MOSTLY D'S: If you answered mostly D's, then your friendship style is long distance. Many long-distance friendships eventually evolve into low-maintenance relationships. However, if your absolute best friend is many miles away, you may want to keep that bond strong despite the distance. Or maybe, you've made a new friend online and you don't want that spark to fizzle out. When it comes to long-distance and online friendships, I've definitely mastered the art of keeping in touch.

I've met the majority of my friends through social media, and they're spread out everywhere—from North Carolina to Connecticut to New York and even London.

TIP: *One of the best ways to stoke the flames of friendship, even through the interweb, is to share a hobby or interest together. I've made pacts with friends to watch movies and then review them together. A friend of mine is a Sims 4 fanatic, and after I picked up the game to see what the hype was about, I fell in love with it too! Now we talk about The Sims nonstop. Another friend sends care packages, and I send TikToks and memes galore. Sending memes is truly the sixth love language, if you ask me.*

Now that my friends have babies, families, and jobs, it's not as easy catching up over the phone. But our text chats keep me thoroughly entertained during my breaks throughout the day. And when they do make their way down south, or me up north, it's like we never spent any time apart.

A REKINDLED FRIENDSHIP

Some friendships aren't necessarily new but are rebirthed in a new season. Whether you've had a falling out or just drifted apart through time, it's always nice to get that old thing back with a good friend. In the Cartoon Network series *Steven Universe,* two of the Crystal Gems, Garnet and Pearl, bump heads after Pearl is caught in a lie that shatters Garnet's trust in her. This results in tension as Garnet gives Pearl the cold shoulder, and Pearl does everything she can to get back on Garnet's good side. After some time, the pair finds themselves trapped by their nemesis in a deadly contraption. They're running out of time and have to work together. Finally, the two are forced to express their feelings. Pearl felt weak and insecure and Garnet felt deeply betrayed. With a new understanding of each other, they're able to work together and escape the trap. The bad guy gets away, but it's alright because the two emerge as closer friends.

Like Pearl, I've had a rekindled friendship in my life, and I'm so happy to have mended the bond I'd broken thanks to my own insecurities. While I wasn't stuck in a literal death trap, the conversations we did have felt just as uncomfortable and definitely nowhere near easy. After explaining what happened and how I felt, my friend took me back with open arms, just like Garnet, and we've been rekindled buddies ever since!

Some connections are worth fighting for, and it's worth it to drop your shield of pride and apologize when you've done wrong. On the flip side, it takes a big-hearted person to hear a friend out and forgive them. I've anxiously dodged many hard conversations, and it always pains me to think what could have happened if I opened my heart and had those tough conversations. Don't let a good friend slip away because of a small misunderstanding.

Not every friendship is worth saving, though. If the falling out was more than a misunderstanding and someone causes you great harm, it's okay to want to keep your distance. After all, you wouldn't unlock your door and let a thief rob you twice! Use your wits and intuition to decide who deserves your magical presence. Making friends is like dating, and sometimes, it just doesn't work. Luckily there are billions of people on this floating rock called Earth and someone out there is a bestie waiting to happen.

WHEN A FRIENDSHIP ENDS

Sometimes friendships finish their season and come to an end. It's not always due to some big falling out, either. Friends can grow apart with time and distance, or by becoming different people due to life circumstances. As powerful as comradery can be, it's also important to surround yourself with friends who can give you as much love, care, and grace as you give to them.

When a friendship is no more, no matter the reason, it can be just as heartbreaking as the end of a romantic relationship. We'll go over how to mend a broken heart in a later chapter, but remember to be kind to yourself. Forgive yourself. And allow yourself time to grieve the lost connection. Don't close your heart off to new friendships, though. Use the tips in this guide to make even more magical connections.

Finding my magical girl gang has been a tough journey for me. I've definitely been through some ups and many downs, but through the power of friendship I've emerged victorious, with a crew of cuties backing me up through every battle. Making new friends is fun, but I can never forget about my day ones who've helped shatter the glass mountain around my heart. Together, we've staved off our Anxiety Monsters, grown through heartbreak, and punched our collective fears in the face.

If I've managed to find comrades to join me in battle, I know you can too! Use the advice I've given you and go out into the world, flying your flag of friendship. The right people will answer your call and the ranks of your magical girl gang will fill up in no time.

Now that we've gone over the power of friends and where to find them...it's time to talk monsters.

HUMP

NOT AGAIN.

YOU PROBABLY DON'T EVEN KNOW WHAT YOUR TALKING ABOUT DO YOU?

WHY WON'T THIS *THING* LEAVE ME ALONE?!

SEVEN

DEFINE YOUR MONSTERS

Magical beings fight monsters! Often, these monsters either feed off of or represent the inner fears that keep us from being our true, shiny selves. In *Miraculous: Tales of Ladybug & Cat Noir*, the main bad guy, Hawk Moth, targets unhappy civilians and "akumatizes" them—turning them into destructive monsters fueled by their negative emotions. One week, a boy feeling frustrated by the restrictiveness of his best friend's father is akumatized into The Bubbler and traps adults in giant floating bubbles all over Paris. Next, a lonely man, Xavier, is berated by a policeman for feeding pigeons in the park. Kicked out of the park and feeling embarrassed, Hawk Moth feeds off of Xavier's sorrow and akumatizes him into Mr. Pigeon—a bird-like villain with the power to control, you guessed it, pigeons. In the first few episodes of *Sailor Moon*, the evildoers take a similar approach. The Dark Kingdom preys on the insecurities of civilians, siphoning energy from young women pressured to conform to society's standard of beauty, and taking advantage of those pining for love.

Just like these fictional monsters, your real-life monsters represent your deepest fears. They target you, prey on your weaknesses, and bring you to your knees by magnifying your insecurities. Grief, confusion, loneliness, impostor syndrome, and the like all act as our personal adversaries, siphoning our energy when we least expect it.

MY MONSTER OF THE WEEK

My monster's been lurking for decades, and he follows me around like a demented shadow. After being pummeled time and time again by his dark aura, I finally discovered the name of my adversary—social anxiety. It's made everything challenging. From friendships to business to little things like grocery shopping, I can never seem to escape its clutches. Just like the Dark Kingdom would cause chaos in the lives of the Sailor Scouts week after week, my Anxiety Monster casts a shadow on everything I do. It's truly my monster of the week.

The first battle I remember with my Anxiety Monster happened when I was five years old. My mother really tried her best to make me a well-rounded young lady. I was enrolled in cheerleading classes, piano instruction, painting courses, church choir, and...ballet. It was actually a tap dance and ballet hybrid program. I remember shaking in my little tutu every time we pulled up to the building. I didn't speak to any of my classmates—I was far too terrified. But over the next few months, we learned a routine to the tune of the "Kangaroo Hop" from Winnie the Pooh and set our sights on the big recital at the end of the course.

By the time the recital came around, we donned our sparkly, blue tutus and shiny, black tap shoes with huge tulle bows on them. We waited backstage as our parents and their friends filled the auditorium. When it was showtime, our instructor lined us up one by one, and to my relief, I wasn't first in line, nor was I last. I was nestled right in the middle. I hoped I'd be lost in the sauce and forgotten. Unfortunately for me, I realized far too late that being in the middle of the line meant being front and center once we arranged ourselves on stage. As soon as I looked out into the dark crowd and heard that first "kangaroo hop!" over the loudspeakers, my Anxiety Monster crawled out of the shadows and struck me with an intense fear. I froze. Then I ran. My little tap shoes pitter-pattered as I darted right off stage, tears streaming down my face.

Over the years, this scene would play out again and again and again. I'd run off many stages in my young lifetime—from church choir to Nigerian cultural events to presentations in class. It was these experiences that taught me the art of disappearing. If my monster couldn't see me, if no one saw me, then I wouldn't be struck down. It was a lonely life, but a safe one. However, there were some things I just couldn't avoid, so I slowly found creative ways to battle my anxiety and survive my humiliation.

In middle school we were tasked with giving a book report presentation in front of our class. I loved reading but hated presentations with every fiber of my being. As I read through the assignment requirements, I could already feel my Anxiety Monster breathing its hot, rancid breath down my back. I shook it off and got to thinking. At the time, I had a bit of an unhealthy obsession with vampires. Not *Twilight*, but films like *Interview with a*

Vampire caught my intrigue, and I had a streak where all the books I read involved tales of the undead. My chosen book of the moment? *Cirque du Freak*.

I decided to add a twist to my presentation and recount the book's plot as one of the characters, Mr. Crepsley—a circus spider tamer and vampire mentor. I purchased a rubber vampire mask from a tiny costume store and...wore it. In front of my entire class. I deepened my voice and told my story, while behind the mask I was drowning in sweat from the hot rubber. Was it embarrassing? Uh, yes, absolutely! I was wearing a rubber vampire mask in front of my thirteen-year-old classmates. But much to my monster's chagrin, I didn't run away. It was then I realized he couldn't reach me behind a mask.

MAGICAL GIRL INTERMISSION

It's time to interrupt our regularly scheduled program to discuss stepping into your magical identity. Magical girls step into their newfound magical identities and use that confidence to defeat their monsters of the week. Don't confuse this for creating a fake persona. Magical girl identities are just the amplification of our truer, most powerful selves.

Although I wore a literal mask to face my fears, what I really did was step into my magical girl identity. I defeated my Anxiety Monster in the moment by amplifying the most magical parts of myself—my creativity and my love for storytelling. I also just so happened to find a way to shield my face in the process.

When faced with your monsters, lean into what makes you feel the most magical. Tap into your power and use your passion to guide you. The glow of confidence and inner magic will cast your monster into the shadows.

Now that I'm older, bigger, and stronger, you'd think I would have already defeated my monster. But no, he's always there and will probably always be there. There are times he grows horrifyingly large, and other times he's small enough to crush under my heel. One recent time he was exceptionally monstrous was during an event when I had to pitch my business to a trio of judges and speak on a panel with a handful of other amazing women. I flew out to another state, on my own, and spent a whole day pacing around my hotel room obsessively reciting my speech over and over again. When I arrived at the event and the time came for me to speak on the panel, I went backstage and sat and waited. I could feel my Anxiety Monster creeping up behind me and waves of slight panic shot through my chest.

A lovely lady with a clipboard, Robin, approached me and asked, "Are you Jacque?" and that's all it took for the floodgates of fear to open. My Anxiety Monster straight up possessed me. He sealed my lips shut and pushed tears out of my eyes. Heat rose to my cheeks and ears, and I felt my vision start to blur. I was having an anxiety attack. I'd never been more humiliated than I was at this moment. Robin fanned me with her clipboard and spoke softly to try and ease my fears. In response to her kind patience, my monster twisted my insides and dug its claws even deeper into my chest. I still couldn't speak. The other women on the panel entered the room one by one. They each took a seat on either side of me and in front of me. They rubbed my back and brought me tea and comforted me. No matter how much they tried to ease my fears, I just could not stop crying, and the more I cried, the more my embarrassment grew.

After what felt like an eternity, it was time for us to go on stage. Once again, we lined up. This time, I knew better than to sandwich myself in the middle. I slid to the back and was the last to walk out on stage. I could hear my Anxiety Monster menacingly laughing in my ear, telling me I was going to screw this up. But I pulled out a trick I had learned back in middle school. I put on my mask. Not a literal rubber mask this time, but one where I projected the person I truly am under all these layers of fear. I smiled widely, told a few jokes, made the audience laugh along with me as I spoke to the crowd about Adorned by Chi and gave business advice to any-one hoping to do the same as me. I was charismatic, albeit awkward, but I was told later it read as endearing. I could feel the pride from the women on the stage, who radiated with supportive energy as they watched me finally open my mouth and speak. When it was all over, I let out a heavy, heavy sigh of relief. My Anxiety Monster slithered away to lick its wounds before its next attack.

> **"Not all of our monsters can be defeated indefinitely, but with time and coping skills they can be wrangled and managed."**

Only a few hours later it was nearly time for my pitch, and I was in its clutches again. I sat alone in a room reciting my speech over and over again. I knew it by heart, but I just kept blanking out. Even though my first experience on stage went exceptionally well, my monster convinced me that it was a fluke. Time passed, and once again I took my seat next to some amazingly kind women who tried to calm my nerves. One woman told me, "Take your phone up there. Even if you have to read that speech off of it—do it."

As the announcer called my name, I felt my entire soul leave my body. I stood behind the microphone, looked out into the dark crowd, and gripped my phone, but I was too scared to look down and read my speech. Instead, the words magically poured out of me. I spoke about not feeling represented, and how I wanted to create something that a little girl could read or watch and see herself in, the same way I saw myself in Janelle Monáe when she danced onto the music scene, declaring herself to be an android. Although I didn't quite command the stage like my peers, I did move the crowd and the judges with my passion and the power of my heart. I left that event winning $10,000 for Adorned by Chi.

> **❝Sometimes we don't know the strength we have until we're in the heat of battle.❞**

While my weekly antagonist may never be truly defeated, I've always found ways to overcome. That is, until the next battle, then I roll up my sleeves, grab my weapons, and get to fighting! And anxiety isn't my only monster either. There've been a few side villains that team up to thwart my inner peace as well. I've battled the Depression Beast, the Thief of Joy, and the Sultan of Self-Doubt, each one sneaking up on me at the most inconvenient times. But with my Heart powers, the support of my magical girl gang, and the guidance of my familiar, I always make it through.

While every magical girl battles different monsters in their life and each battle strategy depends on different factors, I can give you tips from my experience battling my anxiety and depression monsters.

MAGICAL GIRL'S BATTLE STRATEGY GUIDE

The Magical Girl's Battle Strategy Guide is a series of guided questions meant to reveal your adversary, pinpoint how long it's been around, and what you can do to knock it out once it's been identified. The strategy guide includes these three parts:

- Identify Your Adversaries
- Train and Build Your Magical Muscles
- Create a Magical Battle Plan

Bookmark this page. You'll be returning here again as you read through later chapters.

IDENTIFY YOUR ADVERSARIES

The first step to defeating any monster is identifying them. As exciting as it can be to watch a magical girl fight a mysterious, shadowy, no-name villain, in the real world you can't truly charge into battle without first naming your enemies. Be honest with yourself and identify your issues. You'll feel so much relief!

Identifying your monsters can happen in many different ways. I learned about my Social Anxiety Monster after growing tired of hiding in my room and eating junk food to avoid human interaction. I was able to go to a therapist and a doctor, and finally had a name for what I was struggling with. Not everyone has access to either of those resources, though, and there have definitely been times when I haven't. In that case, research is your friend! Head to the internet and search up the details of what you're feeling, find others who share the same experiences, and narrow down what your monster could be. For some, it's depression, for others anxiety, then there's self-doubt, impostor syndrome, loneliness, and even anger issues. Naming what you struggle with will lead to more understanding and a better battle plan.

TRAIN AND BUILD YOUR MAGICAL MUSCLES

Once you've named your enemy, you don't have to rush in and tackle it before you're ready. It's time for a training montage! The prompts below will help you strengthen your magical muscles and create a plan to tackle your monsters.

What monsters are you currently dealing with?
Example: Feeling like an impostor at work.

_____

How does this make you feel?
Example: I feel like I don't deserve my success, and like people are judging my work harshly. My output is suffering. I'm sad and I'm nervous I'll lose my job.

_____

_____

What scares you the most about this monster?
Example: I'm scared that this may negatively affect my work and the worst-case scenario would be losing my job.

_____

_____

How long have these monsters been after you?
Example: I've been feeling this way for the last year.

_____

What caused the initial attacks? (Why do you feel this way?)

Example: Feelings of guilt after getting a promotion. Being overwhelmed with my new workload and difficult changes going on at home.

_____

_____

Let's fight the negative feelings with positive self-talk! List ten things you love about yourself.

Example: My work ethic, my creativity, my positive attitude, my kindness, my resilience, I'm a good friend, I'm a great cook, I've come a long way, and my family loves me.

_____

_____

_____

_____

_____

_____

Now that you've defined your monster and written out your feelings, it's time to make a plan!

CREATE A MAGICAL BATTLE PLAN

I can't give you an extensive, laid-out plan to defeat your monster because you're fighting a battle unique to your own circumstances. What works for one magical being may not work for another, and I don't want to give you steps that may trip you up. What I can do is give you some guidance on how to structure your own plan.

What would life look like without your monster?
Example: Life without my monster would mean being excited about work again and completing my projects.

_____

_____

_____

Now, think of three tangible steps you can take to defeat your monster. List them below.
Example: 1. Alleviate stress at home by asking for help. 2. Open up to my boss about my heavy workload. 3. Call my mentor and ask for guidance.

_____

_____

_____

Is anything stopping you from taking these steps?

Example: I'm nervous to tell my boss that I'm overwhelmed, and I'm hesitant to ask for help because I'm not used to doing so. I don't want anyone to think I'm weak or incapable.

_____

_____

_____

What positives could come from taking these steps?

Example: If all goes well, my boss and family would be understanding of my asks and I'd have a much lighter workload and more help around the house. Both of these outcomes would make me extremely happy.

_____

_____

_____

Reflect on your magical weapon. How can you use your weapon to combat the uncomfortable feelings your monster has left you with?

Example: I can use my magical running shoes to blow off steam at the gym when I'm feeling worn out and overwhelmed.

_____

_____

_____

Excellent plan! Now, list the ways you'll reward yourself after making progress. Battling monsters is hard work, and you deserve to treat yourself.

Example: I'll buy that stunning dress I've been eyeing for months and go to dinner with my friends.

_____

_____

_____

Every magical girl goes through a journey of self-discovery and acceptance, but those journeys aren't always linear. Just like with my experience battling my anxiety, your monster may come back with a vengeance. The return of your foe may be scary, but it doesn't mean you're a failure. Being tripped up can actually become a learning experience that makes you stronger for your next triumph. Just refer back to this plan whenever you're feeling the looming presence of your adversary.

Now that you have a plan of attack and you're taking the steps to punch your fears in the face, with love of course, it's time to wind down and take care of yourself.

EIGHT

SELF-CARE AFTER SAVING THE DAY

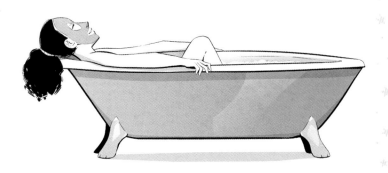

In almost every magical girl series, the plot momentarily takes a tragic turn and things get dark for our protagonists. This chapter is that tragic turn. This will not be a pleasant read, but it's important to understand why I've become so passionate about self-care. While self-care is widely promoted and understood as feel-good routines to boost your mood, and it can be, we often disregard why we need self-care in the first place. The act of self-care is like magical maintenance to combat the heavy stressors of life that wear you down. Just like a car, you put miles on yourself every single day, and you need routine upkeep to keep from falling apart. This is especially important after a tough battle. When the going gets tough, even the most powerful of magical girls need time and space to return to center.

At the end of the first season of *Sailor Moon*, the Sailor Senshi find themselves transported to the North Pole, where they're meant to face off with their unrelenting adversary—the Dark Kingdom's Queen Beryl. When they arrive, they're instead confronted by the DD Girls, five monstrous ladies working under the sinister queen. The DD Girls prove to be more powerful than any monster the Senshi had faced in the past. One by one, the girls are killed off in horrible, violent ways after being tempted with illusions of loved ones. Sailor Moon is the sole survivor, reeling with this horrible loss without the comfort of her support system. Week after week, they'd fought monsters together and always emerged victorious. But this time was different. I've had a similar moment of heart-shattering defeat.

BATTLING THE DUKE OF DESPAIR THROUGH SELF-CARE

One seemingly average Tuesday in June I woke up in a panic. Up until that point, I'd spent months battling with my impostor syndrome while I fought for my voice to be heard. To make matters worse, I'd just discovered I was being misled by someone I deeply cared about. As I struggled, my Anxiety Monster watched from the shadows, licking its chops as it cracked a maniacal smile in the corners of my mind.

Everything I was going through also happened to coincide with the appearance of COVID-19. Suddenly, the entire world was locked down as we all went through a global pandemic together. Seemingly overnight, life was changing in ways I'd never experienced before. I was scared, I was fatigued, and after the tragic murders of George Floyd and Breonna Taylor, I was angry. It was a lot to deal with, and my usual outlets of expression were no longer available to me. I couldn't buy a random plane ticket and escape to more magical pastures for a week. I couldn't drown myself in the hypnotic euphoria of live music. Even something as simple as being enveloped in the calming darkness of a movie theater was out of the question. Instead, I stumbled, bruised and disillusioned, through the tundra that was my life's battleground and called out for someone I could pour my heart out to. But I was devastated to find my friends laid across the wasteland, just as worn down and weary from battling their own personal adversaries—just like the Sailor Senshi.

On that Tuesday morning I laid on my back, wide awake but feeling deeply disconnected from the world around me. I was tired. My Heart powers were depleted. Poor Nala couldn't even get me out of that bed. Hours passed and a strange but somewhat familiar feeling slowly crept up to my chest until it dug its claws into my heart. Before I could grasp what was happening to me, tears streamed down my face and I sobbed. Nala jumped up and tilted her head, scratching at me almost to ask, "What's wrong?" but I just kept crying.

"I can't do this anymore."

Thoughts of defeat bounced around in my head as my lungs tightened and my chest felt caved in by the weight of my despair.

"I don't want to be here anymore."

I didn't know what had struck me. This wasn't the usual blast from my Anxiety Monster's scepter of self-doubt. I didn't have my girl gang to call upon, my defenses were weakened, and battling my anxiety did nothing in this situation. I wasn't strong enough to fight the Duke of Despair.

Time ticked on, but eventually, I had to get up because Nala needed me. When I finally stood to my feet, although it was the middle of the afternoon, my world was blanketed in a thick layer of darkness. Everything moved slower, felt heavier, and looked almost dream-like. Throughout the day, tears streamed down my face like a leaky faucet, no, more like a burst pipe. When the pain I felt became unbearable, I broke down and called my ex-boyfriend, who lived far away in a different city. Usually the more calm, cool, and collected one of my friends, he heard my cries, and I could sense a stark change in his demeanor. He was genuinely worried.

"Call someone to stay there with you," he instructed.

"I don't have anyone to call," I muttered through tears.

"How about calling [Redacted]?"

"Okay..." My words sadly hung in the air like a deflated balloon. [Redacted] was the person who misled me, and it depressed me further that they'd now become my last resort to fight my despair.

Surprisingly [Redacted] did come when I called, and for days they stayed with me as I quietly sobbed. They'd ask me, "What's wrong?" and despair would snatch the words right out of my throat. Instead, I'd only whimper and turn from the embarrassment. Suddenly, on day three, my blanket of sorrow lifted. I felt like myself again, albeit weak and sad. I'd won this battle, barely, but I was worn out and leery of another attack. [Redacted] left once I felt better, and as soon as I was alone, I knew I had to do something to regain my strength. I knew I had to engage in radical self-care.

My radical self-care plan consisted of three parts. The first was immediate, the second was ugly, and the third was my long-term Magical Battle Plan—a self-care routine I'd built over the years, that enchanted all five of my senses.

PART 1: IMMEDIATE SELF-CARE

I made a mad dash for my candles and lit each one with little regard for how the smells would pair together. I just knew I needed to fill my space with nice fragrances. After that, I ripped open a cute, dog-shaped face mask and plopped it on. While I marinated under my dog mask, I readied my Bluetooth speaker and played my absolute favorite Tyler the Creator album—*Flowerboy*. I ordered steak tacos, one of my favorite foods, and pulled up an episode from an old show I adored growing up. The vibes were finally right, and it was time to tap into my power.

TIP: *Your immediate self-care plan should consist of activities you can quickly turn to, to put you at ease. This can be music, your favorite foods, or a nice walk outdoors. Anything you can do to push past those bad feelings in the moment.*

PART 2: THE UGLY

I dusted off my journal and held my magical pen weapon between my fingers. I poured out all of my thoughts and feelings—the good, the bad, and the ugly. And many of them were ugly. I could feel the despair shrinking, just a bit, as I ejected parts of it out of my body and onto the paper.

> **❝** *Build a self-care routine that enchants all five of your senses…* **❞**

Things like lighting candles, using a face mask, or bopping along to your favorite song can definitely make all the difference to a worn-out magical being. But remember, self-care isn't always cute. Sometimes it means ugly crying your eyes out or overcoming discomfort to set a firm boundary with a friend. And sometimes, when you find yourself in the clutches of despair, it means getting professional help.

My ugly self-care plan also consisted of cleaning up after my three-day battle against despair. Once the blanket of sorrow lifted, I looked around and realized I'd completely let myself go. Bills had gone unpaid, and dozens of emails were left unanswered. Clothing was strewn from wall to wall. Containers of half-eaten delivery food orders were stacked up on my dresser. My bathroom looked like a tornado blew right through it, and I wasn't even in Kansas anymore. I was still weak from my battle and working through my recovery, but I knew I couldn't do it in a cluttered, dreary space. So, I rolled up my sleeves and got to work! Was it as nice and pleasant as lighting my candles and watching *Kiki's Delivery Service* for the millionth time? Not at all. But after what felt like an eternity of tidying, scrubbing, and doing other adult things I was extremely pleased with the shiny space before me.

TIP: *When it comes to "ugly" self-care, it's not always easy, but it's always worth it. You deserve to take care of yourself and to live in a space that's neat and tidy.*

> **"** Sometimes when we're knocked down in battle, we can neglect ourselves and it only makes us feel worse. It's okay to take your time and tackle the ugly stuff when you're ready. **"**

PART 3: MY LONG-TERM MAGICAL BATTLE PLAN

For my long-term plan of attack, I turned to my Magical Girl's Battle Strategy Guide, outlined in Chapter Seven, on page 120. I asked myself questions to get to the root of the issue. Why was I suddenly taken unawares and attacked out of nowhere? When did this start? What was I feeling beneath the despair? It was through this exercise that I uncovered the truth—I was dealing with trauma.

The feelings of fear, loneliness, and confusion that come from prolonged trauma are a powerful cocktail of negative energy, and together they have a way of drawing out all of your inner monsters. In the *Steven Universe* spin-off, *Steven Universe Future*, Steven is a magical teen, dealing with the effects of his traumatic childhood—a time spent fighting battles, revealing dark family secrets, and traveling to space, among other life-threatening activities. As a child he was often forced to be the hero time and time again, and now he's permanently wired to be a helper. When the world no longer needs saving, his body reads small problems as major threats to his safety, and he develops strange new powers and a bright pink glow to his skin. Steven eventually sees a doctor, who informs him his new hue is his body's response to his many years of trauma. While my trauma was far less fantastical than escaping a human zoo in space or becoming a creature made entirely of cats, my fear and confusion still mirrored Steven's.

Now that I had a firm grasp on why I was feeling so down, I worked backward and created a to-do list to help pull me out of the depths of despair. The list had steps like "Distance yourself from people who bring you down," "Speak up for yourself, even if it's uncomfortable," and at the top, "Find a therapist." I'd been able to stave off my Anxiety Monster the best I could, but I knew with my Magical Girl Gang down I couldn't handle another visit from the Duke of Despair on my own. So, a few months later, for the second time in my life, I found myself sitting on a therapist's couch.

It was so freeing to discuss how I'd been feeling out loud and without judgment, rather than in the private confines of my journal pages. With each session I felt the color in my life slowly coming back. But soon the costs became too high, and my therapist became a little too invested in my experiences with [Redacted], rather than helping me work through the layers of confusion and despair I felt.

It was incredibly hard to find another therapist that met my needs and stayed within my budget, so unfortunately the most important part of my strategy was delayed. After reflecting on the difficulties I had in seeking help, how all of my friends were as weary as I was, and how mental health and wellness are still an embarrassing struggle for many, I decided to channel my inner Elle Woods. I strapped on my heels, grabbed my textbooks, and headed back to school to become a therapist myself. If I couldn't find the help I needed, I'd become the help I needed! And just like when Usagi embodies the spirit of Princess Serenity and uses the power of the Silver Crystal to defeat Queen Beryl, I called upon my heart power to help me wipe the Duke of Despair from existence.

My dedication to helping others navigate through their feelings has become my newest and most powerful form of self-care. In the past I hated going to school and dragged my feet through it all, but now every assignment and every paper is done with love and hope for my future career as a mental health professional.

MAGICAL GIRL INTERMISSION

It's time to interrupt our regularly scheduled program to discuss burnout. What happens when your passion no longer brings you joy?

In *Kiki's Delivery Service*, Kiki is a young witch who sets out to make a name for herself. Upon landing in a new city, she taps into her inner entrepreneurial spirit and starts a flying delivery business through a local bakery. In order to prove her worthiness as a witch, she overexerts herself and makes many mistakes. Eventually she falls ill and spirals into a deep depression. She loses her ability to fly, she can no longer communicate with her familiar, and she isolates herself from the outside world. She's burnt out.

Luckily, Kiki has her own magical girl gang. She spends time in a cabin with her friend Ursula, an artist who urges her to take her mind off of work and focus on self-care. After some time away, Kiki realizes she's worth much more than the work she does, and she regains her magic. She saves the day, then resumes her delivery business with renewed vigor.

We can all learn something about burnout, self-care, and magic from Kiki's story. It's important not to attach your self-worth to your output or your career. The magic is inside you, after all, so take breaks when you need to and take care of yourself.

Fighting the Duke of Despair was my ultimate magical girl battle. And while I still sometimes feel the effects of its deadly grip, I've been able to create a powerful self-care system to recover after my toughest battles. Keep in mind that every system is unique to the magical being engaging with it. What works for me may not necessarily work for you, but I can share the steps you can take to create a customized super-powered self-care routine.

THE MAGICAL GIRL'S MIGHTY SELF-CARE SYSTEM

- ❤ Enchant Your Five Senses
- ❤ Talk to a Trusted Friend
- ❤ Do the Ugly Stuff
- ❤ Use Your Magical Girl Battle Strategy Guide
- ❤ Recite Your Magical Mantras

STEP ONE: ENCHANT YOUR FIVE SENSES

When you're feeling worn down from battle, it's easy to shut down and disengage from the world around you. That's why it's important to incorporate steps that keep you grounded and engaged with each one of your senses. Here are some examples that I've used for each:

SMELL

Nothing lifts the mood quite like being enveloped in an enchanting aroma. To engage your sense of smell, try lighting candles, using an essential oil diffuser, or taking a shower or bath with yummy-smelling soaps.

TASTE

The warmth and comfort of good food can make anyone smile when they're feeling down. Try eating your favorite snacks or having a comforting meal, drinking tea, or eating sour candy to shock your taste buds awake.

TOUCH

Have you ever felt safe under a nice, soft blanket? It's important to engage your sense of touch during those times you need a bit of comfort. Try petting your magical familiar, squeezing a stuffed animal, or donning a face mask.

VISION

Looking at beautiful or familiar things is always a nice distraction from the monotony of life. Try watching your favorite comfort show, checking out art at your local museum, going for a walk in a nice area, coloring in a coloring book, or painting your nails.

HEARING

Music does wonders for a worn-out soul. When you're not feeling on top of your game, try revisiting your favorite album, playing meditation music, or playing soothing sleep sounds.

Now that you have an idea of what I do, use the space on page 140 to fill out what you'll do when you're not feeling your best and need to engage your senses:

STEP TWO: TALK TO A TRUSTED FRIEND

A magical being's life isn't meant to be lived alone! It's okay to lean on your community of magical beings when the going gets tough. Teaming up to face the forces of evil is what we do, after all. When Kiki loses the ability to fly and talk to her magical familiar, who did she turn to? Her friend Ursula. After confiding in her she gains a renewed sense of purpose. She returns home refreshed, ready to shake off her Depression Monster, and open to embracing her passions once more. This kind of support isn't reserved for fictional magical girls. Here in the real world, we have many people in our lives who are right there, ready and waiting to lift us up out of the pits of despair. Think about the people in your life. Who do you trust with your innermost thoughts and feelings?

_____

_____

Shoot them a message asking if it's okay to share your thoughts and get their input. Leaning on your support system makes all the difference in how you feel and hearing other perspectives can help shape yours. Sometimes when you've been smothered by your monsters, your perception of self is warped, but your friends can remind you of just how amazing you really are.

Talking to a friend when you're feeling down isn't always about venting, even though that's nice to do sometimes. You can simply call to retell old, funny stories or listen to them talk about something they're passionate about. When I'm not feeling my best I love calling a friend of mine who's even more obsessed with cartoons than I am. After an hour or so of discussing how shows like *As Told by Ginger* or *Totally Spies!* inspired our whole personalities and wardrobe when we were younger, I can't help but feel better.

If you don't have your magical girl gang yet or can't think of anyone who will be gentle with your feelings, no worries. When I have fears and feelings that I don't feel comfortable sharing quite yet, I take to the internet to read about other peoples' experiences and how they've dealt with their own monsters. Seeing people overcome depressive moments and triumph through their anxiety helps me immensely and gives me hope. From there it's easy to reshape my current situation in my mind. Perspective shifts are crucial when you're being knocked down by your monsters, as they love to deceive and make you feel worse off than you actually are. After reading through other people's experiences, I talk through my own problems out loud to myself. Just the action of speaking things out loud helps you sort through your thoughts.

Be careful what kind of information you take in, though. While the internet can be a magical place, it can also be a breeding ground for negative feelings and sad souls waiting to be akumatized. Spend time in spaces that have positive, supportive energy. I guarantee you'll feel a little less alone in your struggle.

STEP THREE: DO THE UGLY STUFF

Monsters drain magical girls of their energy, so when you're not feeling your best internally, it tends to reflect on the outside as well. Before you know it, bills have piled up, emails have gone unanswered, and those dishes in the sink are piled so high they're almost towering over you. Traditional self-care with face masks, candles, and nail polish can be cute, but it's often the ugly stuff that makes the biggest impact on your psyche. Although these tasks may not be at the forefront of your mind when you're feeling blue, they do take up significant mental space, and as they continue piling on, it only further weighs you down.

A trick I use to get my life in order after a vicious monster attack is tackling tasks one by one. I'll dedicate one day to each task, and that includes cleaning sections of my space. Thinking of doing it all at once is totally overwhelming but telling myself that the dishes will be done on Thursday, the laundry on Friday, and the bathroom on Saturday makes things feel a little less cumbersome. While you're tidying up your life, listen to a funny podcast or YouTube video. You won't even notice you're scrubbing gunk off a plate when you're busy chuckling to yourself.

When you do manage to tackle the daily tasks you've been putting off, not only will it be a major relief, but your newly cleaned and organized surroundings will entice your sense of sight, touch, and smell as well! Trust me, it's always worth it to do the ugly stuff.

STEP FOUR: USE YOUR MAGICAL GIRL'S BATTLE STRATEGY GUIDE

You can use your Magical Girl's Battle Strategy Guide more than once. Turn back to page 120 when you're feeling down in the dumps, and you'll gain clarity about why you're upset. After you fill it out, you'll have all the tools you need to make a proper plan of attack, then you can tackle each issue one by one until your behemoth monster shrinks into an obnoxious pixie.

Whenever I use my battle strategy guide, I always walk away feeling like I'm more in control of my destiny. While life can sometimes sweep us away in currents we didn't ask for, we can always use paddles to steer ourselves in another direction.

STEP FIVE: RECITE YOUR MAGICAL MANTRAS

Speaking kindly to and about yourself is one of the most important things you can do when you're not operating at one hundred percent. The world is cruel enough, and bad guys are vicious enough. You don't want to mutate into your own personal monster. Hype yourself up! You should be your own biggest fan. Recite these magical words, out loud, to feel like your best self again:

- ❤ "I'm loved and cared for."

- ❤ "I deserve all of the good things that happen to me."

- ❤ "I'm magical and powerful."

- ❤ "I have the power to defeat my monsters."

- ❤ "The world needs someone like me!"

- ❤ "I'm worthy of kindness and compassion."

- ❤ "I belong in every space I find myself in."

- ❤ "I am loved, and I am valuable because I exist!"

- ❤ "The universe is on my side."

Feel free to add more mantras to the list in the space on page 145.

Now that you have your mantras, speak these words out loud, say them in your head, or write them on your bathroom mirror in lipstick if you have to! Soon enough, they'll transform into positive pink energy that cuts down your menacing monsters.

I told you this would be a tough chapter, but here you are on the other side of it with more magical tools at your disposal. I'm so proud of you. Now it's back to our regularly scheduled programming. Let's hit the reset button and talk about your magical beauty routine.

NINE

THE MAGICAL GIRL'S BEAUTY ROUTINE

*T*his chapter will be a short one because you're already a beautiful being, and there's not much I could tell you to improve on the perfection that is you. Seriously. Day in and day out, we're inundated with messages that we're not beautiful enough, smart enough, slim enough, tall enough. And I'm here to tell you, you are enough, and you are worthy of being treated with care. The world needs you, regardless of how you look. And trust me when I say you look good—so embrace that!

When it comes to discussing beauty standards, there's an episode of *Sailor Moon* that stands out to me. Usagi's upset because she's gained weight. Rather than encouraging her to love herself as she is, Luna surprisingly taunts her and draws an image of her with a much larger body. Suddenly, all of her friends and classmates are obsessed with losing weight. Their teacher, Ms. Haruna, is looking noticeably slimmer, and the girls learn that she's been attending a new state-of-the-art gym—Shapelin. What they don't know is that Shapelin isn't a real gym, it's a setup for the Dark Kingdom to drain energy from unsuspecting young women. While her friends workout, Usagi is suffering from a new "diet" she's been trying and ends up passing out, which is frightening. When she comes to, her crush Motoki tells her he prefers curvier women. Now, armed with her newfound boost from a crumb of male validation, Usagi doesn't mind how she looks, and she finally consumes food, only to run into Mamoru and Luna, who both taunt her for her eating habits. Sailor Moon does save the day in the end, but her body image issues remain.

This episode saddened me, not because everyone was getting the energy sucked out of them, but because our main magical girl doesn't realize just how beautiful she is. And for the brief moment she's okay with her looks, it's only because of the words of a man. *Sailor Moon* isn't the only series to cover weight loss and body image in this way. In the Korean series *Flowering Heart*, the students at Ari's school are obsessed with the new transfer student's looks. She's "slim and beautiful"; meanwhile, Ari is struggling with her self-confidence after discovering a single pimple on her forehead. At the same time, students are being weighed for a school-wide physical evaluation. The girls all stress about their appearance, including a student named Juyeon, who feels extra pressure to lose weight. Juyeon enlists our main magical girl Ari, and her friends, to help her exercise, and all the girls decide to go on a diet together. Tubby, Ari's magical hamster familiar, tries to explain to Ari that there's no need being so obsessed with her looks, but she brushes him off.

Juyeon eventually abandons her diet, not because it's difficult, but because she's sad about a boy she likes transferring schools. More male validation driving characters' motivations. Ari's friend Min laments over not being able to help Juyeon, which triggers the emergence of her magical girl power. She then transforms into an adult personal trainer. Yup. A whole magical transformation only to step out of her shiny light in a sports bra, because she wished she could help Juyeon lose weight. While I love magical girls and their lessons of friendship and love, messages like these could be harmful to anyone who needs to hear that they're okay just the way they are.

Luckily, there are shows that divert from this way of viewing food and health. An example is in the series Tropical-Rouge! PreCure. In episode 8, the Cures, our main magical girls, spend the whole day learning how to cook well-rounded meals to help out around the house. They're so into their new hobby that they forget to eat, so when a monster comes around wreaking havoc, they're too famished to fight. The girls take a break from battling to eat and nourish themselves. There's no dieting here—only listening to their bodies and making choices that make a positive impact on their vitality and strength levels. Afterward, they have enough energy to take down the bad guy! This to me is a cute, wholesome way to teach lessons about health and food. In the end the girls are happy, healthy, and still kicking monster butt while adorably dressed.

HOW TO GAIN YOUR INNER MAGICAL GIRL GLOW

While we all know that magical girls are the epitome of beauty, it's not because of how they look. Their immaculately styled hair and perfectly pleated skirts are easy on the eye, but what makes them really shine is that inner magical glow. It's the way they stand up for their friends, show compassion to their enemies, and stand up for love and justice. Usagi never needed to starve herself, and her classmates didn't need to feverishly work out to embrace their inner beauty. Usagi is an open-minded and supportive friend with a big heart. That's what makes her beautiful.

Because I don't want you to fall into a cycle of self-loathing fueled by society's impossible beauty standards, I'll be giving you tips and tricks to finding that inner glow we all have inside, and, of course, a few beauty hacks I've picked up along the way. Although we don't need makeup, nails, and hair to be beautiful, they're all still fun! Just remember, the packaging matters very little once the gift inside is revealed.

MAGICAL GIRL INTERMISSION

It's time to interrupt our regularly scheduled program to discuss magical girl glow-ups. Magical girls go through stunning transformation sequences and emerge in beautiful, hyper-feminine 'fits. Think pleats, frills, and bows galore! And don't forget the glamorous gloves and boots. Not only is there an outfit change, but they also manage to paint their nails and lips and do a full face of makeup in under a minute. It's really quite impressive.

Magical girls don't go through all of that for the approval of men or romantic prospects. They glow up to become more powerful, to embrace their magic, and to help their friends. These transformations make the girls more glamorous but also more terrifying for their enemies, who know what's waiting for them after all the sparkles and lights dissipate.

Learn to see your own transformation in the same way. You're not glowing up to get the guy or girl. Instead, you're embracing your magic and driving your enemies into the shadows with your terrifying, otherworldly glow. You're stepping into your power and emerging a more confident, magical, and happier you.

Your inner glow is what sparks the transformation sequence that makes you look brilliant and powerful on the outside. Sometimes, when you're feeling down and dull, it can take a lot of effort to buff yourself and get that radiance back. In times like those, rest up and tackle the dullness when you're ready. Once you are ready, here's what you can do.

SMILE TO YOURSELF IN THE MIRROR: The simple act of smiling actually releases endorphins, aka happy hormones. Not only does smiling make your brain happy, but it's also contagious and can trigger grins from the people around you. That's why it's important to smile to yourself even when no one else is around. Also, it's been proven that smiling is super attractive. This is the beauty chapter, after all!

PRACTICE GRATITUDE: While life is definitely hard, it's important to set aside time to express gratitude for the parts of life that make you smile. Keep a journal where you jot out a daily list of positives, or you can recite them out loud. The more you focus your energy on the vibrant parts of life, the more fulfilled you'll feel. And when you're feeling down and out, you can whip out your journal and become reacquainted with all the things you love.

DRINK WATER: Another simple activity that improves your mood and appearance? Drinking water. Water lubricates your joints, helps deliver oxygen throughout your body, and flushes away toxins. Along with being physically good for you, drinking plenty of water can actually lower your risk of anxiety and depression.

GET ENOUGH REST: Imagine our favorite magical girls charging into battle with heavy bags of sleep under their eyes. Imagine them facing off against the monster of the week while yawning. Imagine them swaying, weighed down by exhaustion, during their transformation sequences. Magical girls need rest to recharge and energetically face the day.

EAT A HEALTHY MEAL: Just like the Cures from *Tropical-Rouge! PreCure* did, it's important to nourish your body so you can face off with your monsters at full capacity.

You don't want your monster to growl at you and your stomach to growl back. It can be easy to let the day get away from you when you're a busy magical being, but always remember to eat when you're hungry.

DANCE AROUND: Physical movement also ups your happy hormones. What better way to get your body into motion than through dancing? Turn up your favorite song and have a one-person dance party right in your bedroom. Bonus points if you teach yourself a dance routine!

MEDITATE: Because we live in a noisy, chaotic world, meditation can feel strange at first. It's hard to disconnect from the outside world and look inward. But it's so important to take quiet moments throughout the day to simply be, without the pressure to perform or take up space.

CHECK ON A FRIEND: Nothing makes your soul glow quite like checking up on a friend with no expectations. Just good vibes and a loving exchange of magical energy. Try reaching out to a friend you haven't heard from in a while. They'll be so happy to see your name pop up in their notifications!

VOLUNTEER: Donating your time and resources to people in need is an amazing way to make your spirit glow. There's nothing quite like seeing a warm smile spread across a stranger's face where there wasn't one before. I've mentored a little one through Big Brothers Big Sisters, volunteered at a women's shelter, and even created my own organization in college, giving back to children in need. Each of these experiences filled my heart with a sense of purpose. While they were challenging and heavy at times, knowing I was making a difference made it all worth it.

STAY IN YOUR MAGICAL LANE: There's nothing more magical than minding your own business. Sometimes we get so wrapped up in what everyone else is doing that we lose sight of who we are inside. Always keep your eyes on your own road, because you're on a wonderful journey that deserves your full attention. If you find yourself swerving into another magical being's lane, hit that turn signal and dip right back into yours.

SHOUT YOUR MAGICAL GIRL BATTLE CRY: Magical girls kick off their transformations by shouting out their battle cries and bathing in a shower of light. When they emerge, they're posed to perfection, their nails are painted, their hair is shiny, their makeup is on point, and their battle fashions are runway worthy. When it comes to your magical girl battle cry, it can be whatever makes you feel good! Marinette Dupain-Cheng calls out "Spots on!" to transform into Miraculous Ladybug and, of course, we all know when we hear "Moon prism power makeup!" that Sailor Moon is afoot and it's about to go down.

Personally, I love to look in the mirror and say, "I am loved, and I am valuable because I exist!" No, there's no showering of light that totally transforms me, but there is a warm feeling that rises up to my chest and envelopes my heart. Your battle cry helps you face the day with your best face forward. What will you choose as your daily battle cry? Write it out in the space below.

_____

_____

_____

HOW TO TRANSFORM YOUR APPEARANCE

Now that you're happy, hydrated, and full of positive inner vibes, it's time for your outer transformation sequence. Here are a few ways you can make your outside appearance match your inner beauty. Because I'm a lover of saving money, these tips will be cost-effective as well.

TAKE A LONG SHOWER OR BATH: When I'm feeling dull, a regular shower just won't do! Nothing makes me feel more magical than a long, steamy shower. I take my sweet, sweet time and light candles, then I lather up with fancy-smelling soaps and go the extra mile with my skin care routine. Once I'm done, I finish it off with a yummy body butter. If you prefer to bathe, toss a bath bomb and some essential oils in your bath water. If you're feeling really fancy? Add rose petals and truly treat yourself to a magical experience. When you emerge from the depths of your shower, you'll feel fresh and beautiful.

PRESS-ON NAILS ARE YOUR FRIEND: I used to drop over $60 every two weeks on my nails. I love the whole process of getting my nails done, but honestly it was getting costly, so I looked for other ways to pretty my fingertips up. That's when I took a new interest in press-on nails. I actually don't press them on, I glue them on, file down the rough edges, and in less than thirty minutes and for less than $10, I've become a polished goddess. It's also a pretty peaceful process and one of my go-to self-care rituals. Do they last as long as my salon nails? Definitely not! But for those few days, I feel like a princess. If press-on nails aren't your thing you can always use nail strips or simply paint them yourself!

WIGS, WIGS, WIGS!: Wigs are a fun, quick, and affordable way to elevate and switch up your look. When I want to emulate the sleek glamour of '70s Cher, I pop on a black, bone-straight wig. If I want to channel my inner magical girl, a pink curly wig will do. You can truly become an entirely different person with a $50 wig.

BEAUTY SUPPLY STORE MAKEUP IS A-OKAY: Let me let you in on a secret. I'm definitely a Fenty fanatic when it comes to my foundation, but for everything else, I frequent my local beauty supply store. They truly are a wealth of affordable beauty products. For years, I've utilized my local beauty supply store for concealer, liquid eyeliner, and juicy lip glosses. Why break the bank when the outcome looks just as glamorous?

PICK YOUR SIGNATURE SCENT: When you smell good, you feel good, and when you feel good, you look good! Grab your favorite perfume and spray it on your neck and wrists. You don't need a pricey scent to smell like a million bucks. Places like Bath and Body Works have an amazing selection at an affordable price.

EXPERIMENT WITH YOUR FASHION: Every once in a while, it's fun to shake things up style-wise! Over the years, I've learned how to maximize my pieces and squeeze a ton of outfits out of a very minimal clothing selection. My number one tip for getting your bang for your buck? DIY. Back in college, I took my mom's sewing machine and learned how to make simple alterations. I made skirts shorter, turned long tops into crops, and nipped baggy pants at the waist to make them sleeker.

If you don't have this skill, or don't want to learn, that's okay! You can DIY without a single needle and thread. Some long skirts can be instantly transformed into dresses, simply by pulling them up and belting them at the waist. Or a wrap dress can be unwrapped and worn as a long flowy cardigan.

Accessories can also elevate an outfit. A simple white tee and jeans can be transformed with strappy heels, layered necklaces, and a bright cross-body bag. Think Telfar's bubblegum pink mini. It's up to you and your imagination!

If you're in need of a closet overhaul, try hitting up a thrift store. Places like Buffalo Exchange and Goodwill have classic and trendy pieces you can incorporate into your wardrobe without spending an arm and a leg.

If you're thinking of a complete style overhaul or need help crafting a look that speaks to your soul, a good place to start is Pinterest! About once a year I create a new Pinterest board to represent my personal style. I add images of outfits and aesthetics I really love and after about a week, I start to see recurring patterns and pieces. Then, I buy those pieces and patterns and style them on myself in my own unique way.

One month I found myself drawn to off-the-shoulder princess sleeves, so I tracked down as many pieces as I could with this cut. This led to an entire month spent dressed like a Renaissance Fair actor, and I couldn't have been happier!

The beautiful thing about being a magical being is you don't have to stick to any one look. You can change your outfits with your mood, experiment with your style, and let your creativity run wild.

MAGICAL GIRL INTERMISSION

It's time to interrupt our regularly scheduled program to discuss the magical girl outfit changes in *Cardcaptor Sakura*. In the series, Sakura bypasses the traditional magical girl transformation sequences.

Instead, her best friend Tomoyo creates a new custom 'fit for each battle.

Tomoyo had our girl Sakura in billowing capes, colorful berets, big bows, and pom poms galore! My absolute favorite costume of hers was a futuristic, angel-inspired outfit. It's pink, it's topped with a winged headband, and she looks straight out of a scene from *The Jetsons*. Not to mention the practical white boots. Love!

The lesson to be learned here: Don't be afraid to step out of the box and try new battle-ready outfits to match your mood. Not only will it confuse and dazzle your adversaries, but you'll also put them to shame fashion-wise.

Add these transformative tips to your daily beauty routine and you'll see a major difference, not only in how you look but how you feel inside. Now that you're all shiny and cute, it's time to talk about romance.

TEN

FINDING LOVE AFTER FIGHTING CRIME

*F*inding love isn't easy for anyone—even if you've got magical powers. There are lots of confusing love triangles, frustrating misunderstandings, unrequited crushes, and major heartbreaks. Sailor Moon finds Rei (Sailor Mars) dating Mamoru, who's actually destined to be with Usagi. Then there's *Miraculous: Tales of Ladybug & Cat Noir*, where our two heroes are in a frustrating love triangle, erm square, with their own alter egos. But as much as love can sometimes hurt and confuse us, it's also a beautiful, magical experience.

I like to call myself a reluctant hopeless romantic. I love love, but I'm oh-so-sensitive and hate getting my heart broken. While I've had some great luck with love, just know I've also dealt with some major f*** boys too. Through my experiences I've learned so much about what to do, what not to do, and what not to accept in any dating situation. So, magical being, if you're looking for advice on finding love after fighting crime, look no further!

MAGICAL GIRL INTERMISSION

It's time to interrupt our regularly scheduled program to discuss being vulnerable with your heart. In the 2005 series *Sugar Sugar Rune*, Chocolat and Vanilla are two tween witches vying to become the next Queen of the Magical World. The two best friends are gifted amulets and wands then sent to Earth to collect human hearts, guided by their rock star mentor Rockin' Robin. Whoever collects the most hearts becomes the next Queen.

The caveat is the girls cannot give up their own hearts to anyone. While humans have an almost unlimited supply of emotion-induced crystal hearts, witches have only one. So, if things aren't done properly, love will literally kill them. Romance for a witch instead includes a mutual exchange of hearts, but a betrayal of that love exchange would mean, you guessed it, death. Those are some high stakes, and it makes sense that the girls would be hesitant to fall for anyone.

Luckily, here in the real world, us magical beings are not bound by these life-threatening rules. Sometimes we give up our hearts and what we receive in return doesn't live up to our expectations. Sometimes others give us their hearts and we're not ready to receive them. Other times both hearts shatter in the process, and we're left to pick up the pieces. The beauty in this is with each failed exchange, we have the ability to learn and grow. So, by the time we exchange hearts with our true love, both are gleaming with passion and perfectly crafted by our life experiences.

It's scary to be vulnerable with your crystallized heart, but it's so worth it in the end.

DATING DO'S

Here are several dating do's that magical girls should keep in mind:

HAVE OPEN COMMUNICATION: It's so important to have the freedom to be emotionally expressive with your partner. A relationship is more than date nights and warm, fuzzy feelings. There will be misunderstandings and hard times, and you'll have to be able to communicate to solve issues. If you find yourself feeling frustrated, walking on eggshells, and unable to express your feelings, it's worth evaluating if your partner deserves your magical presence.

Many magical girl relationships go through hardships due to lack of communication. In *Sailor Moon*, when Mamoru has clairvoyant-like nightmares about Usagi's future death, he attempts to change that future by coldly breaking up with her without explaining himself. When she inquires further, he says it's because she's weak. Ouch. Then, sixteen episodes pass before things are cleared up. Had Mamoru been honest with Usagi about his fears from the beginning, maybe all the heartache, tears, and awkwardness could have been avoided.

Some people find it hard to communicate. Maybe they've been socially conditioned to keep their feelings bottled up, or they've been treated harshly when they have in the past. It's important to be patient, lead by example, and speak your mind clearly, but gently. Let your partner know that openness is important to you, and express your own feelings with "I" or "we" statements, rather than making them feel like they're the problem. Here are some examples of ways you can introduce open communication into your relationships:

"Hey, I've been feeling a disconnect and wanted to talk through things to make sure I'm understanding your feelings."

"I've been feeling a bit disappointed by how much time we spend apart. Could we make time for a date this weekend? I love hanging out with you!"

"I've noticed you've been looking a bit down. Is that true?"

Remember, you can only do so much. If your efforts to communicate are continually brushed aside and you feel on edge and misunderstood, maybe the person you're dating isn't the one for you. You also deserve the same patience and kindness extended to you.

KEEP UP WITH YOUR FRIENDS AND FAMILY: It's easy to become so intoxicated by feelings of affection that you neglect your other relationships, but your romantic connection isn't the only one that matters. The love from your friends and family holds just as much importance as love from a partner—if not more. Remember, it's your magical girl gang that's been fighting by your side as you battle monsters. Until your new beau proves they're in for the long haul, be careful not to make them your entire universe. A little space can be healthy, and it's true that absence makes the heart grow fonder.

In *Winx Club*, Darcy, one of the series' villains, drives a wedge between Riven and his friends by sabotaging him during a race and blaming it on Bloom, one of the Winx Club fairies. She feeds into his insecurities and frustrations and makes him doubt the loyalty of the people he's closest to. This manipulation leads to the pair dating and Riven betraying his friends for his new girlfriend. This is a major red flag! If someone is methodically isolating you from your support system, that's a definite sign of a more sinister plot. Narcissists and abusers often use this tactic to make their targets more vulnerable and easier to manipulate. A good way to weed these bad apples out is to maintain a healthy balance of time spent across all of your relationships.

TRY NEW THINGS TOGETHER: Shared experiences bring people closer together, and it's always cool having a partner in crime to try new things with.

For most fictional magical girls, like Sailor Moon or the ladies of the Winx Club, growing closer to their beaus means sharing traumatic experiences, like battling beasts or being revived after death and reincarnated. But for us real-world magical beings, it could be as simple as watching a new show together or as extravagant as an island getaway.

My advice is to start small. Going on vacation with anyone can strain a connection if it's not already strong. Try things like food festivals, concerts, and hands-on activities like cooking classes first.

BE A MIRROR FOR YOUR PARTNER: The world is full of our own personal monsters, mean-spirited people, and overwhelming challenges—so why not do everything you can to make your partner see how incredible they actually are? Be a mirror for the person you love so they can see the best parts of themselves reflected back to them. Tell them what you adore most about them. Pick up a few of their hobbies and connect with them through something that makes them happy. It's worth it for creating a closer, more positive bond, but it's also enough just to see them smile. Some people may not appreciate your gestures, but the right one will.

Looking back to another scene from *Sailor Moon,* there's an episode where Usagi bakes cookies for Mamoru. Not only does she clumsily drop some, every single one is burnt. She cries and feels like she's failed as a future wife, since she can't seem to live up to the domestic goddess she'd like to be. Mamoru recognizes that she only wants to make him happy, and in a sweet scene, he tries the cookie and tells her that he accepts her for who she is. Later, Usagi happily tells her friends how Mamoru ate every single cookie, and they're shocked he didn't get sick. This is a great example of Mamoru being a mirror for Usagi. He recognizes her effort and care, and reflects that back to her, rather than highlighting her blunder. This is what good partners do!

Being a mirror isn't a one-sided effort, either. As much as you pour into your partner, they should do the same for you. When dating, look for people who give as much as you do, who show interest in the things you love, and whose words match their actions.

Now that you know these crucial dating do's, here are some red flags to be aware of.

DATING DON'TS

When it comes to dating, of course there are don'ts. Here are some behaviors in yourself and others that you should steer clear of:

LEADING WITH THEIR EGO: Relationships shouldn't be full of egotistical mind games. I've been in situations where, rather than openly communicating, we've played a game of "who can ignore a text message the longest." By then you're so tired of the game that the conversation never happens and the spark fizzles out. It always stands out to me when someone's willing to solve a problem right then and there rather than letting their ego ruin a good thing. The right person for you will be mature enough to lay down their ego and say what they mean to move things forward in a positive way.

LEADING YOU ON: Not every spark grows into a flame. Sometimes the connection just isn't there, even if there was an initial attraction. That's perfectly normal! But the moment a person realizes their interests have changed, they should be up front and honest about it. In *Sailor Moon*, Mamoru and Rei (Sailor Mars) casually date, but it's clear the "relationship" is one-sided, with Mamoru showing little interest in the fiery girl he's spending time with. Instead of dragging this fake situation, he should have let her know from the start that his feelings didn't match hers.

Leading someone on can be so damaging to their self-esteem. And when a person finally gets fed up with themselves and leaves their partner in the dust, they'll be heartbroken and left wondering what went wrong. As hard as it is to break someone's heart, it truly shatters if you're strung along and left with no answers. While being open about changed feelings is truly the right thing to do, not everyone operates in this way. When you sense a shift in a person's interest level, pull away. Spare yourself from the frustration of romantic confusion. If their intentions eventually become clearer, and you really like them, then you can try again.

GROWING TOO ATTACHED: In *Miraculous: Tales of Ladybug & Cat Noir*, Marinette has a crush on her friend and partner in crime-fighting, Adrien. She takes her affection a bit too far by breaking into his locker, stealing his phone, and having a calendar in her room with his schedule plotted out so she knows where he is at all times. And, well, I'll just outright say it: it's super weird and not okay!

Your partner should know that you are a person with a mind and time of their own, and they have to respect that. You're two different people choosing to share space with one another. A relationship doesn't equal ownership. Remember to continue maintaining your own routines and your own life outside of your romantic relationship. If you feel your partner becoming too attached, try encouraging them to spend more time with friends or to pick up a hobby.

BEING AFRAID OF HEARTBREAK: This one's for you! Fear of heartbreak holds us back from so much. It stops some from expressing their true feelings and others from dating at all. But if you're so afraid of heartache that you never experience the beauty of love and affection, is it really worth the avoidance? We all want our happy endings, but every journey to the Land of Love includes a few bumps in the road. And in our individual chapters of romance, sometimes the happy ending is the breakup. Breaking up hurts, and the pain you feel is similar to the grief of losing a loved one, because you are losing a loved one. But remember you're better off single for some time than stuck in a confusing, toxic, or one-sided relationship.

MAGICAL GIRL INTERMISSION

It's time to interrupt our regularly scheduled program to discuss toxic relationships. In *Winx Club*, Musa, one of our main fairies, and Riven, our previously mentioned friend betrayer, are in a turbulent on-again, off-again relationship.

Riven is a "bad boy" with an often prideful attitude, and he and Musa argue and bicker over misunderstandings, jealousy, and more over the course of their multi-season relationship. With every toxic coupling, there are moments of magic that shine through the bleakness and make it easy to forget all the toxicity that happened just ten minutes prior. This is definitely the case with Musa and Riven, as the pair seem hooked on the feeling of making up after breaking up.

While love is an important factor for every magical being, often the healthiest love they experience is between themselves and their friends. When it comes to romance, Musa's situation isn't out of the ordinary. Many fictional magical beings find themselves stuck in either a frustrating love triangle, a one-sided relationship, or a turbulent one like Musa and Riven's. But us real-world magical beings can break the spell of unhealthy affection and work toward building genuine, healthy bonds.

Being destined to be together isn't enough if you're not dropping your ego, communicating, and being open to receiving love. Sometimes breaking up is the best thing you can do!

BREAKING UP IS HARD TO DO

After each breakup I've had, there's been a lengthy period of mourning. It's hard losing someone you shared so much with, no matter how it ends. Just like when Mamoru savagely dumps Usagi and she's left to pick up the pieces alone, my first real heartbreak felt like my world was crashing all around me.

I met my first boyfriend in college after a mutual friend mentioned knowing another Nigerian, and I swiftly added said Nigerian on Facebook. I shot him an innocent message, and we chatted for a bit, but it didn't go anywhere. That is, until I ran into him in real life at a TJ Maxx and the butterflies in my stomach did backflips.

After staring for a few seconds too long, I took a deep breath and approached the object of my affection as he browsed for affordable jeans.

"Hey, do you know who I am?" I smiled.

"Oh, hey, yeah!" He returned my smile.

My heart felt like it was going to shoot through my chest and hit him in the face. I never dated or dealt with the male species in any capacity before college. I had no clue how to end the conversation or where to take it beyond my awkward giggles. Luckily for me, he asked for my number, and that was my cue to hand it over and make my exit. Once I got to the car I melted into my seat and smiled from ear to ear. High school me would never approach a cute guy in a TJ Maxx, but I was a bold, new, more magical Jacque.

> **Don't be afraid to shoot your shot! You never know what will come of it. Be bold, magical being.**

Soon, we were studying together, and before I knew it, I had a new boyfriend. At first, it was a bit strange, and I didn't know what to do with him. He'd call me "babe," and I'd correct him—"Uh, my name's Jacque." And he'd ask me for simple favors only for me to snap at him for asserting dominance, because I didn't want any man on this planet telling me what to do. In reality, he had a hole in his pants pocket and I owned a sewing machine, so it only made sense to ask. Eventually, I dropped my tough exterior and opened up to him about my secret cyber life. I braced myself for the barrage of embarrassing and judgmental words he was sure to throw my way, but instead he shrugged and asked, "What's so weird about that?"

That simple, indifferent question changed everything for me. He didn't find my blogging weird, he supported my entrepreneurial ideas, and he found interest in things that were important to me. And through it all, I remained perplexed. Either this guy was extremely strange, or I wasn't as strange as I felt. Both things were true. But thanks to his warm, nonchalant acceptance, I opened up more and more. I'd wear my huge hair and suits and Oxfords both on campus and on dates with him, and he never batted an eye.

❝No matter what, there's someone out there who will love and appreciate all of the things that make you magical.❞

Unfortunately, our relationship ended a bit after college. Although I was the one who chose to close that chapter, I was still devastated when it was all over. But after some time and a lot of support from my friends, I was able to move on. Fast forward to now, and there's no bad blood between us. Because we were communicative, we both realized we were simply young and inexperienced at love. I'll never forget that he helped me out of my shell and made me feel accepted, loved, and seen, even when I tried my hardest to disappear. For that I will always be thankful.

Breakups may feel like the end of the world, but really they're the start of a new chapter. You had the chance to experience sharing love with someone else, which is incredible! And with everything you learn in the process, imagine how much more magical your next connection will be.

HOW TO GET OVER A BREAKUP

Breaking up is never easy. Now that it's just you again, there are several things you can do to get back on your feet.

BE KIND TO YOURSELF: No matter what side of the breakup you're on, it's easy to continually blame yourself as you mull over what went wrong or wonder if you made the right decision. It's natural and helpful to reflect on your past relationship, but if it gets to the point where you're beating yourself up, remember to ease up and be kind to yourself. Everyone makes mistakes; there's not a perfect person on this planet. Give yourself the same grace you'd extend to a person you love.

PICK UP NEW HOBBIES/PASSION PROJECTS: Nothing's more exciting than picking up a new hobby or trying out a new activity. Now that you have more you-time, you can try all the things your ex may not have wanted to do. You also have much more space on your calendar to pursue your passions. Do you have a book you've been wanting to write? A business idea that you've been itching to kickstart? Now's the time!

SPEND MORE TIME WITH FRIENDS: Spending time with friends is the perfect medicine for a broken heart. Being around people who love, value, and care for you truly helps to heal your heartache. This is why I've continually stressed the importance of friendships. Relationships can go as quick as they come, but a bond between good friends is much stronger.

BLOCK OR MUTE THEM: If you ever get the urge to see what your old flame is up to, it's better to block or mute them so you can move on more quickly. Even if you ended the relationship on good terms, trust me, it still hurts to see glimpses of their life that you're no longer part of.

Cutting off contact speeds up the heart-healing process exponentially. You can always unblock once you've gotten over your breakup. So, what are you waiting for? Hit that shiny red block button!

WRITE OUT YOUR FEELINGS: If you haven't noticed, writing is my solution for almost every problem. This should come as no surprise since my magical weapon of choice is a pen. In my experience, feelings are easier to sort through when they've been written down. Then you can reflect and learn from what you've noted. Get all those gross feelings out of your body and onto the paper!

SELF-CARE IS YOUR FRIEND: Self-care is a crucial component of breakup recovery. When you find yourself nursing a broken heart, refer back to our Self-Care after Saving the Day chapter.

BE OKAY WITH THE PROSPECT OF NOT GETTING CLOSURE: When you're dealing with a breakup, you may want answers from your former flame. Why did they break it off? What did you do wrong? What could you have done better? But the thing about feelings is they don't make any sense. You can't make sense out of something that's abstract and random. People are often confused by their own actions, so pressuring them to make sense of their feelings through tears and heightened emotion could be pretty difficult. You have to accept that you may never get closure, not because it's being withheld, but because your former beau might not have the answers you'd need.

Know that your heartbreak is valid, and it sucks, but it won't last forever. You'll emerge from the fog of sadness stronger, wiser, and with a heart that's ready to connect to another's again. But while you wait, remember to give yourself a little extra love.

FINDING LOVE WHEN YOU LEAST EXPECT IT

Magical girls love love and can find it anywhere. Seriously, that beautiful barista at your local coffee shop could be your reincarnated soulmate from another dimension. And that obnoxious coworker who's always trying to one-up you could end up staring back at you lovingly as you walk down the aisle. After I technically met my first boyfriend at TJ Maxx, I knew love could for sure be found among discounted menswear and affordable shoes. But my next boyfriend proved that love could truly be found in any place you could imagine.

After my first serious breakup, I threw myself back into my online life. This time, I became a lot more familiar with Twitter and used it to connect with other business owners and cartoon lovers. One day I logged into my email to find a mysterious, faceless man had sent me a message, saying he'd seen my tweets and wanted to hire me for a social media job. Mind you, at the time my Twitter was unrefined and super random, but I was flattered that I must have come across polished and professional. I was also broke, so I agreed to chat. In hindsight, this may not have been the smartest idea, so tread carefully if you ever find yourself in a similar situation.

Anyway, we hopped on a phone call to go over the tasks he needed done, but I was instantly enamored by his voice. As he described the plans he had for his business, I snapped out of my love haze long enough to catch a major opportunity he was missing. I outlined what he should do instead, and he was amazed at my plan. I was beaming with pride over my genius idea.

For our next meeting, I requested video. For all I knew, he could've been a cutthroat criminal on a government watch list or a creepy old man living halfway across the globe. But I just had to attach a face to that voice. To my surprise, when the video popped up, a handsome young Ghanaian man was staring back at me.

"Oh! Wait...so you're not an old man?"

He laughed. "You thought I was some creep, huh?"

I nodded my head, and he laughed again. I ended up abandoning the project because I was attracted to him, and that would've been weird. After two months of texting nonstop, I flew out to his state so we could meet in person.

I was smitten from the minute we met. I ended up visiting him three more times back to back and I told all my friends back home about my mysterious new beau.

We shared ideas and grew our businesses together before parting ways due to my anxiety. He tried his best, but his logical mind couldn't rationalize my illogical fears, and we ended up breaking up due to incompatibility. I learned a lot of lessons from him that I still carry with me now. He made me feel more confident in my business prowess, and I'll always think of him fondly.

> **"Love doesn't always happen in conventional ways. Romance can find you when you least expect it."**

Romance doesn't always go the way you would expect. You may have imagined bumping into your crush at a bookstore and caressing their fingers as you both reach for the same copy of some obscure novel you've been meaning to read. Or maybe locking eyes with your soulmate from across a crowded concert venue. But you could also meet them when you're barefaced and shopping for socks or when you're both leaving laughing emojis in the comment section of an Instagram meme page. Love is random in that way. But that's what makes it so magical.

> **"Sometimes romance requires a second, third, or fourth try. In a world full of billions of people, you're bound to meet your match!"**

SELF-LOVE IS THE BEST LOVE

Although I'm currently dating someone, I've decided to focus on something we often push to the side in lieu of pursuing romantic relationships: falling in love with myself! My relationships have been mirrors where I've seen my most endearing and admirable traits reflected back to me through the eyes of my partners. My partners loved my resourcefulness, my creativity, and my laughter. If they could fall in love with those parts of me, why couldn't I? The same question goes for you.

What do others love most about you?

Example: My smile, my caring nature, my corny jokes

Now, what do you love most about yourself?

Example: I love my creativity

I'm not one of those people who say, "In order to find love, you have to love yourself first." That's simply not true. We're all works in progress, and there's no magical Valhalla of self-love where you're deemed fit to date. I met my past partners when I was at my worst, and they loved me through it the best they could even after our romance was over. None of the time we spent was a waste, and I learned so much about compassion, compromise, and care. You should love yourself, not to attract a partner, but because you're simply amazing, and not loving yourself just won't do. Your mysterious side-character-turned-love-interest will come. But in the meantime, romancing yourself is a must!

HOW TO ROMANCE YOURSELF

Use the tips below to court yourself and add a bit of romance to your life. No partner necessary.

GET ALL DOLLED UP: I love getting all dolled up, even when I have nowhere to go. Dressing up and getting cute for yourself gives you a major boost of positive energy and confidence. You get extra points for sharing selfies for your friends to gas you up. Go ahead, put on your absolute favorite outfit, do your makeup how you like it, or don't wear any at all! The point is to look good so you feel good, and what that means is totally up to you!

TAKE YOURSELF ON A DATE: This is something I've started doing in the last year or so. I've packed up a blanket, wine, and snacks, and read a comic at the park, then took myself shopping. It was a little awkward being alone with my thoughts, at first. I thought after some time I'd learn to appreciate the quiet...but I didn't! Instead, I put on some headphones and vibed out to my favorite tunes while I spent the day with myself. Everything's better with a soundtrack. With music to inspire your mood, you can pretend you're the star of some indie coming-of-age movie exploring a new city. Need some self-date ideas? I've got you!

● **See a movie solo:** While it's fun to have movie nights with other people, it's incredibly relaxing to watch a movie by yourself and enjoy the action without someone else whispering commentary in your ear. Plus, you won't have to share the popcorn!

- **Dine out on your own:** Head to your favorite restaurant with a book and grab a table for one. You'll be able to enjoy your food at your own pace while taking in the sights and sounds around you.

- **Cook for yourself:** Get creative and try out a new recipe, then plate it like you're Gordon Ramsey serving royalty at a five-star restaurant. You'll be proud of yourself for creating a tasty dish that's fit for a queen or king!

- **Have a picnic:** Grab a blanket, make a sandwich, and pack some wine, then head to your nearest park! This is a great way to enjoy the outdoors, and if you pick the right location you may even make some new friends.

- **Go shopping:** Go shopping at locally owned bookstores and boutiques for a unique experience that helps the local economy.

GAS YOURSELF UP: Speak as kindly to yourself as you would a romantic partner. Tell yourself how beautiful, kind, and compassionate you are. Compliment your smile, your laugh, that little thing you do with your eyes. Embrace yourself. Tell yourself you're the most magical being to ever walk the Earth. The more you say it, the more you'll believe it and the more confident you'll feel!

SURPRISE YOURSELF: I love ordering surprise gifts for myself online. I'll preorder something that I know will take a few weeks to a month to arrive, then I'll forget about it. That way I'm pleasantly surprised when a mysterious package is waiting for me at my doorstep.

Love can be messy, confusing, and even scary, but it's worth it to open your heart and experience the magic that comes with romance. And remember, love isn't exclusively shared between two people in a relationship. You can romance yourself, share intimate moments with friends, and spend quality time with your family. Heartbreak is almost inevitable, but even the grief of breaking apart a bond can lead to lessons learned. Go out into the world with an open heart. You've got this!

OUTRO

Well, magical being, it seems our time together has reached its end. It's bittersweet, isn't it? As we've learned, magical girls aren't all about cute costumes, sparkly transformation sequences, and giggling with their friends over their latest crush. They fight horrifying monsters who often feed off of their inner fears and insecurities. They deal with loads of loss and the grief that comes with it. Then there's the heartache from breakups and unrequited love. And through it all, they manage to maintain a healthy social life, even if they mess up from time to time.

Magical girls embody the strength that lies in femininity, friendship, and love, but this doesn't mean they're perfect. Usagi is a crybaby, Marinette can be insecure, and Steven Universe struggles with his desire to rescue everyone around him, but it's these imperfections that make them all the more magical. Being able to stare down a horrifying monster while shaking with fear and uncertainty, yet still defeating them with the power of friendship is an incredible feat. Magical girls often struggle with impostor syndrome, just like we do, and they costume up and save the day regardless.

In the world of magical girls, nothing's more powerful than the bonds of friendship. While one magical girl can be powerful on her own, when she teams up with her loyal companions, their magic knows no bounds. Not only do they take down bad guys together, but they also support each other off the battlefield—giving advice, partnering up to study, and discussing their dreams and their futures together.

As you've learned throughout this guide, here in the real world, our magic is much more subtle. It lives under the surface, making quiet appearances that you may miss if you don't know what to look for. In our world, the mundanity and injustices of life distract us from embracing our own inner magic, and our monsters are invisible adversaries who attack our hearts and minds. But if you're reading this, you've stepped into the most magical version of yourself, and you know where to look to find those moments of positivity, hope, and possibility in the chaos and adversity that surround us. You've found your familiar, and you've taken hold of your weapon. All with your magical girl gang by your side.

Facing your monsters is no easy task, but through this journey you've taken them on with style and a fist full of magical force. You've created an enchanting self-care routine that you can whip out when you've grown weary from battling your weekly antagonist, and you've explored the romantic side of being a magical girl as well.

You also now know a bit, perhaps far too much, about me. My ultimate hope is that you've learned something from my stories, from growing up awkward to taking on my magical girl mantle to finally knocking down my Anxiety Monster. But at the very least, I hope they entertained you!

I started on this path as your familiar, guiding you through discovering your power and declaring your magical moniker. Now I'm ending our journey as a permanent member of your magical girl gang and a forever friend. In the beginning, I asked if you'd ever dreamed of becoming a magical girl, and now here you are, standing before me as a powerful, luminous warrior of love and friendship. I'm so proud! And I'm so happy you answered my call.

But before you fly off with your weapon in hand, remember, you are worthy. You are loved. You are beautiful. And you deserve all the good things that happen to you. I can't wait to see you out on the battlefield, fellow magical being. And just know I'll be right there beside you, cheering you on.

XOXO,
Jacque

P.S. Nala also says hello!

MAGICAL GIRLS YOU SHOULD KNOW

I mention a few series throughout this guide, but there are so many more magical stories out there! Here's a list of shows and books that you should check out:

- Adorned by Chi
- *Agents of the Realm*
- *Bee and PuppyCat*
- *Cardcaptor Sakura*
- *Flowering Heart*
- *Kiki's Delivery Service*
- *Sailor Moon*
- *MagnifiqueNoir*

- *Miraculous: Tales of Ladybug & Cat Noir*
- *Princess Love Pon*
- *Sleepless Domain*
- *Star vs. the Forces of Evil*
- *Steven Universe*
- *Sugar Sugar Rune*
- *Winx Club*

THE OFFICIAL MAGICAL GIRL GLOSSARY

We've gone over a bunch of new terms and sayings! If you need a refresher, check out the Official Magical Girl Glossary below:

Akumatized: In *Miraculous: Tales of Ladybug & Cat Noir*, the main baddie, Hawk Moth, uses akumas to transform emotionally distressed civilians into super-powered villains to do his bidding.

Anxiety Monster: A hulking beast that preys on the fears of magical beings across the globe. It pops up in times when you need confidence and rips it to shreds. He can be battled with support from your magical girl gang, magical mantras, and professional treatment.

Duke of Despair: A harrowing monster that feeds on the misery, sadness, and defeat of its host. It often rears his ugly head when there's trauma around. It can be battled through self-care, self-awareness, and professional treatment.

Familiar Discovery Tool: A series of questions meant to help you discover which category of magical familiars is meant to guide you on your journey.

Magical being: Not all magical girls are "girls"! The term "magical being" encompasses all people living the magical girl lifestyle.

Magical familiar: A tiny talking creature, infused with magic and wisdom, that guides our magical girl through life and battle. Familiars in the world of magical girls often approach first. In the real world, we pick our own familiars.

Magical girl: Weapon-wielding, cute-costume wearing, crime-fighting cuties! They're often accompanied by an anthropomorphic furry familiar and together they fight bad guys in the name of friendship and love. Not every magical girl is a "girl." Any magical being can don an adorable costume and fight! Examples of magical girls include Sailor Moon, Cardcaptor Sakura, and Miraculous Ladybug.

Magical girl battle cry: The statement you want to shout to the world before charging into battle. For Sailor Moon, it's "Moon prism power, makeup!" Ladybug's battle cry is "Spots on!" As a magical girl in the real world, your battle cry is whatever makes you feel shiny inside.

Magical Girl Battle Plan: After your training montage, it's time to make a plan of attack. Your Magical Girl Battle Plan is a list of action items you create, based on the current monster of the week.

Magical Girl Battle Strategy Guide: A series of guided questions meant to reveal which adversary is attacking you, how long they've been around, and what you can do to knock them out once they've been identified. Includes a training montage and your Magical Girl Battle Plan.

Magical Girl Identifier Index (or MGII.): A series of questions meant to help you identify which power category you best fit under.

Magical Girl Name Generator Questionnaire: A series of questions meant to guide you toward uncovering your magical girl name.

Magical weapon: Items like wands, staffs, and heart-shaped compacts. In the real world, we can find magic in the things we use every day. For example, my magical weapon is a pen. I use it to build worlds and craft stories—like this book. To put it simply, weapons are just useful, personalized tools to concentrate and redistribute your inner power out into the world.

MGII: An abbreviation of the Magical Girl Identifier Index.

Monsters: Creatures that feed off of our inner fears. Week after week, they swipe at us, hoping to knock us down. Unluckily for them, you're now equipped with this guide! This book contains a multitude of secrets that they don't want you to know about.

Self-care: Magical girl maintenance. Weary magical girls need upkeep, and self-care consists of ways you can return to center after a tough battle.

Social anxiety: The irrational fear of social situations. Anything from giving a speech to meeting someone new can trigger anxiety attacks and racing thoughts.

The Grayness: The boring mundane that surrounds our everyday lives. Almost everything we do is to add color to our lives and escape the grayness's blah clutches.

The Master Manipulator: An unhinged genius, using the power of its mind to mix things up in yours. Friends become foes and love becomes contempt when he's around.

The Real World: There's the fictional world of magical girls that exists in black and white manga pages or on glowing TV screens. The real world is our current perception of existence. We often perceive the real world as rote and mundane; however, there are flecks of magic beneath the ordinary, everyday surface.

The Sultan of Self-Doubt: A cunning monster that burrows his way into the minds of magical beings, casting illusions of mediocrity and making them doubt their own power.

Transformation Sequence: During a magical girl's transformation sequence, they're enveloped in a sparkly shower of light. Once they step out, they've transformed into their most magical self. This includes a beautiful costume, hair done, nails done, and makeup on point. During this transformation the magical girl also becomes super powered.

Trauma: An emotional response to a disturbing or upsetting event.

ACKNOWLEDGMENTS

I'd like to thank my family and friends for supporting me and sticking with me through the shiny times and the periods of dull lulls. Your love has gotten me through so much, and I could never call myself a magical girl without you all!

Thank you to my mom for being my biggest fan. Thank you to Rachel for being my partner in crime (fighting). Thank you, Victoria, my fellow *Sailor Moon* fan, for helping me stay focused on my goal. Thank you, Diana, for the constructive advice.

Thank you, Casie, for seeing that shiny spark in me and allowing me to write this book. Thank you, Tyanni and Renee, for being magical editors.

Thank you to the people I've loved who taught me many lessons. Thank you to the people I've worked with along this journey.

Thank you, Venus, for the lovely artwork. Thank you, Kristine, for the cute logo.

And thank you, reader, for trusting me with your magical girl journey!

ABOUT THE AUTHOR

Hey there, I'm Jacque Aye! I'm a Nigerian American therapist-in-training and founder of the Adorned by Chi lifestyle brand.

Since launching Adorned by Chi in 2015, I've worked with the likes of Sanrio, collaborating on a collection for their Small Business, Big Smile initiative, and my brand has been sold at Hot Topic! As a member of the online manga and anime space, I've grown my small, tight-knit community into one that boasts over 100,000 magical beings across social media.

I'm a vocal supporter of mental health awareness and self-care among Black women, and I advocate for those suffering from social anxiety. In 2020, Adorned by Chi was able to donate $10,000 to the Loveland Foundation's Therapy Fund.

Catch up with me on my personal website and shoot me a note if you need me at www.jacqueaye.com. You can also find self-care playlists, including one specifically curated for this guide, on my Spotify account. Look me up! And stay magical.